ADVANCE PRAISE FOR *California Foundations of Education*

"I enjoyed how accessible and useful this is for teacher candidates and even faculty. This text is critical to the work we do to prepare socially- and politically-aware educators. Noel succinctly captures the historical and contemporary foundations of K12 education in California that weaves in pertinent issues of race/ethnicity, culture, and language. The use of reflective and action-based discussion questions make this an essential read for K12 educators and teacher education faculty."

Patricia D. López, Ph.D.
Assistant Professor, California State University, Fresno

"*California Foundations of Education* is an outstanding effort to provide a clear, competent, well-organized history of schooling and education in California, with particular attention to the evolution of politics and policies that has shaped and re-shaped formal public education throughout the state's history. The book is an essentially significant contribution to those preparing teaching professionals for work in California schools. It is a critical analysis of the evolution of educational policies that frame teachers' and students' roles and responsibilities in the historical and contemporary context of public education. Dr. Noel's book would be an invaluable resource in teacher education/credentialing courses, as well as graduate courses in foundations/history/politics of education in California. I could see where this book might be considered an adopted foundational text in schools of education. Required reading."

Thomas G. Nelson
Professor of Curriculum Studies and Teacher Education
University of the Pacific

"Jana Noel's book explicates the forces that have shaped California's educational system—and in turn California itself—in profound ways. She illustrates how the beliefs and actions of people and policymakers in communities and in the courts play out in materially important ways, from the earliest days of Statehood with its nascent public school system, to its 19th and 20th century struggles and strivings to expand educational opportunities to non-white children, right through the more recent days of A Nation at Risk, NCLB, the ESSA act, and including current issues related to school choice and privatization. The scope of the book is sweeping: she clarifies how policies arise and are shaped by subsequent legal decisions, tackling big-ticket issues such as how schools are funded, who controls budgets, who decides what gets taught (and what gets left out), what gets assessed, who gets certified to teach, and how all of these issues relate to equity and social justice in a state that has seen more change demographically, socially, and economically than any other state in the union. Any serious student of the history of education in California—and indeed the history of California more generally—will find this work illuminating."

Grinell Smith, Ph.D.
Professor, Connie L. Lurie College of Education
San José State University

CALIFORNIA FOUNDATIONS OF EDUCATION

Myers Education Press

Published by Myers Education Press, LLC
P.O. Box 424
Gorham, ME 04038

Myers Education Press is an academic publisher specializing in books, e-books, and digital content in the field of education. All of our books are subjected to a rigorous peer review process and produced in compliance with the standards of the Council on Library and Information Resources.

LIBRARY OF CONGRESS CATALOGING-IN-PUBLICATION DATA AVAILABLE FROM LIBRARY OF CONGRESS
13-digit ISBN 978-1-9755-0217-1 (paperback)
13-digit ISBN 978-1-9755-0216-4 (hard cover)
13-digit ISBN 978-1-9755-0218-8 (library networkable e-edition)
13-digit ISBN 978-1-9755-0219-5 (consumer e-edition)

Printed in the United States of America.

All first editions printed on acid-free paper that meets the American National Standards Institute Z39-48 standard.

Books published by Myers Education Press may be purchased at special quantity discount rates for groups, workshops, training organizations, and classroom usage. Please call our customer service department at 1-800-232-0223 for details.

Cover design by Sophie Appel.

Visit us on the web at **www.myersedpress.com** to browse our complete list of titles.

CALIFORNIA FOUNDATIONS OF EDUCATION

Educational Development Within a Diverse Social History

BY JANA NOEL

Myers Education Press

Gorham, Maine

Acknowledgments

I want to thank Chris Myers, founder of Myers Education Press, for the opportunity to publish this book. I would also like to thank Stephanie Gabaree and the rest of the Myers Education Press staff who helped put this book into production. My appreciation also goes to Grinell Smith, San Jose State University, who served as a reviewer and provided helpful feedback during the process of developing the book's direction.

On a personal note, I want to give special thanks to my husband David Powell and to my parents Jim and Jan Noel, all of whom have given me love, support, and encouragement not only while I was working on this book, but in all my personal and professional endeavors.

Table of Contents

INTRODUCTION:

Diverse from the Start

The diversity of California's people pre-dates its statehood. First, many Native American tribes were spread throughout the land that became California. It is estimated that before Europeans arrived in North America, one-third of all Native Americans in what is now the United States lived in the area that is now called California (Starr, 2005). By 1769 there were 310,000 Native Americans in the state's lands speaking more than 100 languages (Dutschke, 2014). In addition to the many Native American tribal governments, five different national flags have flown over portions of what is now California: England (for 37 days in 1579), Spain (1542, then again from San Diego to San Francisco from 1769 to 1821), Russia (at Fort Ross on the Northern California coast, from 1812 to 1841), Mexico (1821–1848), and the United States (1850–present). When word arrived in 1822 that Mexico had seceded from Spain, California pledged allegiance to Mexico. California remained a part of Mexico until the United States, in the Treaty of Guadalupe in 1848, took the Mexican land following the bitter Mexican-American War. In 1850 California became a state. Due to its Spanish and Mexican origins, California's Constitution was written in both Spanish and English. The California Constitution also declared California a non-slave state, although it restricted the rights of Blacks and others to fair treatment. Add to this diverse history the Gold Rush, in 1849, and California became the designation for the largest migration in the history of the United States. While the non-native population was around 100,000 at the time, the Gold Rush attracted nearly 300,000 people from the rest of the United States including Blacks and Native Americans, and around the world, from countries such as Peru, Chile, Mexico, China, France, Russia, Italy, the West Indies, and Australia. Clearly, California had become incredibly diverse.

With its newly designated status as a state in the United States, with its history as a destination for people from multiple national origins and racial backgrounds, and with its economic potential due in large part to the Gold Rush and trade routes, California began developing a system of free public education. Not all was smooth or equitable, however, as the prejudices and legalized restrictions against various racial, ethnic, and nationality groups were also evident in the development of education in California. From government boarding schools that contributed to the loss of Native American culture and life, to separate Chinese schools and "colored schools" that were legally segregated schools for Chinese and Black children, to Mexican schools designed to keep Mexican children segregated, California has provided an uneven system of education throughout its history.

Demographics in California's Public Schools

According to the U.S. Department of Education, there were just over 50 million children nationwide in K-12 public schools in 2017–2018. Meanwhile, the California Department of Education reported over 6 million children attending over 10,000 K-12 public and public charter schools. This means that 12% of all children attending public schools in the United States are in California. The demographics of California students and teachers can be seen in Table I.1. Note that the terms used here come directly from the California Department of Education, and they do not represent all racial, ethnic, or national groups *(see Table I.1 on page xiii)*.

Additional demographic information from the California Department of Education (CDE) show further diversity within California's schools.

- 61.5% of California's K-12 students are "socioeconomically disadvantaged," a category describing students who are eligible for free or reduced-price meals, or who have parents or guardians who did not receive a high school diploma.
- 42.3% of students speak a language other than English in their homes, either as a primary or second language. Sixty-five languages are spoken by California students, with Spanish spoken by 85% of second language speakers.
- 20.4% of students are English Learners, a category of "students who are learning to communicate effectively in English; typically requiring instruction in both the English Language and in their academic courses" (California Department of Education, 2018 [CDE]).

Table I.1
Ethnic Distribution of Public School Students and Teachers: 2017–2018

Ethnicity	Number of Students	Percentage of Students	Percentage of Teachers	Number of Male Teachers	Number of Female Teachers	Total Number of Teachers
African American not Hispanic	340,841	5.5%	3.9%	3,705	8,457	12,162
American Indian or Alaska Native	32,500	0.5%	0.4%	464	1,047	1,511
Asian	569,744	9.2%	5.6%	4,023	13,227	17,250
Filipino	151,650	2.4%	1.4%	1,171	3,380	4,551
Hispanic or Latino	3,376,591	54.3%	20.2%	16,834	44,921	61,755
Pacific Islander	28,920	0.5%	0.3%	281	687	968
White not Hispanic	1,442,388	23.2%	63.3%	51,131	142,065	193,196
Two or More Races Not Hispanic	219,429	3.5%	0.8%	722	1,907	2,629
None Reported	58,350	0.9%	3.6%	3,086	7,995	11,081
Total	**6,220,413**			**81,417**	**223,686**	**305,103**
				26.7%	**73.3%**	

https://www.cde.ca.gov/ds/sd/cb/ceffingertipfacts.asp

Note: Adapted from Fingertip Facts (2018).

Teacher demographics have been included in Table I.1 because, simply stated, teachers matter. As the data show, the only demographic group of students who are fairly likely to see a teacher of their own race or ethnicity is White students. The likelihood of California students of color seeing their own ethnicity represented in their teachers is low: students of color make up 76.8% of the total student population in California, while teachers of color comprise only 36.7% of the total teacher population. While this is larger than the national data on teachers of color, which is 19.9% (National Center for Education Statistics, 2017), California still has a mismatch between students and teachers. As can be seen in Table I.1, there is also a higher percentage of female (73.3%) than male (26.7%) teachers throughout K-12 education.

Purpose of This Book

As I teach courses in Educational Foundations, I am constantly struck by the lack of attention paid to the development of education in California within the currently available Educational Foundations textbooks. In many cases, students have not been asked to consider how education might have developed within California. As we work our way through the traditional texts, I have begun asking my students questions such as the following: How has the unique diverse social history of California impacted the development of its public schools? Did California have legalized school segregation? Is there anything about the political structure of California that may have an impact on education that is not discussed in traditional texts? How are textbooks selected in California? By simply raising questions such as these, we can encourage students to gain a better understanding of how California's K-12 educational system developed and currently functions. The main focus of the book is on how education in California has developed in relation to the unique diverse social history of California.

Traditional textbooks rightfully provide a national perspective on the U.S. educational system, describing issues from many different viewpoints to represent as much of the U.S. educational system and society as possible. The organization of this textbook is structured by the similar topics as traditional textbooks, but approaches every topic by focusing on education in California, and especially how that is impacted by California's diversity.

Organization of This Book

The chapters that follow include information about the educational system in California. Each chapter begins with a set of Guiding Questions to focus the reader on key topics in the chapter. Each chapter also contains a section on issues of equity and social justice, although these issues tend to be woven throughout the educational system in California and are thus integrated throughout the chapters. Finally, each chapter concludes with a section on Reflective and Action-Based Questions, designed to elicit further reflection on the topics in the chapters and to suggest actions that can be taken to tie the information in the chapter to the practice of education in schools and society.

This book is organized similarly to commonly used Foundations of Education textbooks that describe education at the national level. Following this Introduction, there are eight chapters laying out and discussing the wide range of Foundations of Education, specifically related to California.

Chapter One: History and Purposes of Education in California lays out the development of the public schools of California within the complex set of ideologies, prejudices, and economic development in the state, including historical purposes of education, laws, separate schools for children of color, the development of a system of teacher education, and the beginnings of curriculum in the state.

Chapter Two: Political Influences and Organizational Structure of Education in California has two focal points: the influence of politics on education, and the way that education is organized within California. All of this is surrounded by national reform movements and California's responses. The chapter also includes a discussion of the ways that communities can be involved in the political process surrounding education.

Chapter Three: Funding Education in California describes the complex nature of how schools are funded, including the ongoing struggles to provide equitable funding for all schools in the state. The chapter lays out funding formulas, court cases and propositions, and how the state over time has impacted differentially students of different racial, national, linguistic, needs levels, and income levels.

Chapter Four: Curriculum, Content Standards, and Instructional Materials discusses how California's curriculum addresses the various national reform movements over time, including discussion of power and privilege in curriculum adoption. The chapter describes the state standards and curriculum frameworks for each subject, and also provides readers with the methods to critically analyze curriculum for potential bias.

Chapter Five: Assessment and Accountability: Practices and Issues both describes and critically analyzes the assessment and accountability movement at the national level as well as California's responses, including the development of new policies and practices as well as the concept of high-stakes testing. The chapter also provides data on the impact of economic status on test scores as well as efforts to reduce and ensure equitable testing for all students.

Chapter Six: Immigration and Language Polices in California Education, discusses both immigration patterns into the state and language policies and laws, with the purpose of providing readers with the history, current framework, and an understanding of support organizations that assist teachers in providing improved education for English Language Learners as well as recent immigrants into California.

Chapter Seven: Family and Community Engagement, encourages the reader to learn about the large array of community-based organizations, public agencies, nonprofit organizations, parent groups, and businesses providing services that enable a more complete education than can be offered by the school alone. Teachers and future teachers can enhance their own relationships with their students by learning about, and hopefully becoming involved with, community organizations that support their school.

Chapter Eight: The Teaching Profession, California Style, wraps up the chapters by taking the reader through the process of earning a teaching credential, becoming a teacher, and continuing to learn as a teacher. Finally, three Appendices point the reader toward key documents and organizations that provide the framework for education in California: the Education Code, the California Department of Education, and the California Commission on Teacher Credentialing.

References

California Department of Education. (2018, July 10). *Fingertip facts on education in California—CalEdFacts*. Retrieved from https://www.cde.ca.gov/ds/sd/cb/ceffingertipfacts.asp

Dutschke, D. (2014, October). A history of American Indians in California: Introduction. *Five views: An ethnic historic site survey for California*. Retrieved from http://ohp.parks.ca.gov/pages/1054/files/american%20indians%20in%20california.pdf

National Center for Education Statistics. (2017). *Digest of education statistics. Table 209.10: Number and percentage distribution of teachers in public and private elementary and secondary schools, by selected teacher characteristics: Selected years, 1987–88 through 2015–16*. Washington, DC. Retrieved from https://nces.ed.gov/programs/digest/d17/tables/dt17_209.10.asp?current=yes

Starr, K. (2005). *California: A history*. New York: Modern Library.

CHAPTER ONE

History and Purposes of Education in California

Guiding Questions

1. *How was education embedded as an integral part of California from the time of statehood?*
2. *How did educational law treat different groups of children differently based on race?*
3. *What does "Americanization" mean in K-12 schools?*

Introduction

The creation of the public school system in California was based on a complex set of ideologies, prejudices, economic development, and efforts on the parts of many communities and educators who believed that education was critical to the development of the children of California. Unlike many states in the East that became states before the concept of free, public education became accepted, the concept of state-supported schools was created at the very outset of the formation of the state of California. Although based on the diversity that created the state from its inception, California also legalized segregation of children into separate schools. This chapter covers the development of the public schools of California, including historical purposes of education, laws, and separate schools for children of color.

Creating a Public School System: 1850–1900

The creation of a free, public school system was critical to the development of the state of California. Many aspects of K-12 education were considered at the initial point of statehood, but the system would take years to develop, and it is still evolving today. In particular, as the diversity of the state's population grew, California schools promoted Americanization as well as separate schools based on race.

Education in the California Constitution

The concept of free public education had been developing in many parts of the United States prior to California's statehood, so California was able to incorporate public schooling into its earliest formation as a state. As Hendrick (2000) explains, "the national model of public schools was established before 1848 and would eventually apply to California as well" (p. 226). The establishment of a state-supported school system in California was a part of the California State Constitution, Article IX. This article set the purposes for such an educational system, the amount of time the schools would be open, the administrative structure of the state schools, how school funding would occur, and the punishment to be meted out if a school district did not set up schools appropriately. It even considered the spectrum of education, proposing the idea that California's education would eventually include a public university *(see Figure 1.1 on page 3)*.

New England's Influence on California Schools

The influence of New England philosophy of education on the creation of a free, public school system in California is undeniable. The vision of a free, publicly supported system of common schools set out by Horace Mann, and adopted throughout a wide area of New England, can be seen in the legislation, the debates, and the reports of educational leaders in California during the creation of the public school system from 1850 to 1900. In fact, the first free, public school in the state of California was in San Francisco in 1851, and was created by a Board of Education that was comprised entirely of people who had moved from New England. *(For more information about Horace Mann and his influence on education, check the PBS series "Only a Teacher. Schoolhouse Pioneers" at http://www.pbs.org/onlyateacher/horace.html.)*

The most important part of this New England influence was the belief that public schools were essential. In January 1852, the first State Superintendent of

FIGURE 1.1 - ARTICLE IX OF THE CALIFORNIA CONSTITUTION

Article IX of the California Constitution

SECTION 1. The Legislature shall provide for the election by the people of a Superintendent of Public Instruction, who shall hold his office for three years, and whose duties shall be prescribed by law, and who shall receive such compensation as the Legislature may direct.

SECTION 2. The Legislature shall encourage by all suitable means the promotion of intellectual, scientific, moral and agricultural improvement. The proceeds of all land that may be granted by the United States to this State for the support of schools which may be sold or disposed of, and the five hundred thousand acres of land granted to the new States, under an act of Congress distributing the proceeds of the public lands among the several States of the Union, approved A.D. 1841, such per cent as may be granted by Congress on the sale of lands in this State shall be and remain a perpetual fund, the interest of which, together with all the rents of the unsold lands, and such other means as the Legislature may provide, shall be inviolably appropriated to the support of common schools throughout the State.

SECTION 3. The Legislature shall provide for a system of common schools, by which a school shall be kept up and supported in each district at least three months in every year; and any district neglecting to keep and support such a school, may be deprived of its proportion of the interest of the public fund during such neglect.

SECTION 4. The Legislature shall take measures for the protection, improvement, or other disposition of such lands as have been or may hereafter be reserved or granted by the United States, or any person or persons, to the State, for the use of a university; and the funds accruing from the rents or sale of such lands, or from any other source, for the purpose aforesaid, shall be and remain a permanent university, with such branches as the public convenience may demand, for the promotion of literature, the arts and sciences, as may be authorized by the terms of such grant. And it shall be the duty of the Legislature, as soon as may be, to provide effectual means for the improvement and permanent security of the funds of said university.

Public Instruction, John G. Marvin, wrote in a report to the legislature about the importance of gaining public support for the burgeoning free, public schools:

> From data of a reliable character, there will be a large emigration of families the ensuing year who design making our State their permanent home. It is to be hoped, therefore, that the State, as well as parents, will perceive the deep responsibility resting upon them and speedily furnish the facilities for organizing and sustaining a system of free common schools. (Ferrier, 1937, p. 67)

First Public Schools

The earliest public schools were developed in Northern California, most likely as a result of the heavy influx of immigration due to the Gold Rush and the trade routes set up through the river system and ocean port cities. Table 1.1 gives the population of the 10 largest counties by population in 1852 (from Ferrier, 1937, p. 67).

TABLE 1.1 - 1852 CENSUS OF COUNTIES

El Dorado	40,000
San Francisco	36,157
Yuba	22,000
Nevada	21,365
Calaveras	20,192
Tuolumne	17,657
Sacramento	12,589
Placer	10,784
Mariposa	8,969
Butte	8,572

The first free public school was established in San Francisco in 1851. While the school opened with only three students, within a year there were 300 students. By 1853, there were three free public schools located within San Francisco. Public schooling was created in other cities as well, but at varying rates. Overall, in the state by 1852, there was a combination of some public schools, some private schools, and some places that had no schools (see Table 1.2). In Calaveras County (mining territory) there lived 100 children, but there was no school in the county. San Luis Obispo (central coast) reported 200 children with no school. With 400 children reported in Sacramento County, only 3 schools existed. In order to have education for their children, many locations resorted to either private schools with tuition or education provided by Catholic and other religious orders, including schools in Monterey, San Rafael, San Jose, Napa, and Santa Cruz (Hendrick, 2000).

Table 1.2 - Years That Schools First Opened

San Francisco	1851
Stockton	1853
Oakland	1853
Los Angeles	1853
Sacramento	1854
San Jose	1856

Purposes of Education—Americanization

A main purpose of the schools at the time was to "Americanize" students into the developing American style of intellectual literacy and morality. The framers of the California public school system did not just want children to be able to attend school, they wanted children to gain the attitude and morality that they deemed to be "American." A story from the newspaper *The Pacific* illustrates these sentiments. The story was written one month before the first public school opened in San Francisco in 1851.

> We want schools which shall be as free to all classes of the community as the air we breathe. We want American schools which shall train the rising generation for the duties and the responsibilities of American citizens . . . the State is destined ere long to occupy a position of most commanding influence and importance. But in order to accomplish this all her institutions must be American in all their essential characteristics. (Ferrier, 1937, p. 54)

John Swett—"Father of the Public School System of California"

As public schools continued to open across the state, free schooling became available to more and more students in California (although still only to White children). When John Swett was elected State Superintendent of Public Instruction in 1863, the number of free schools in the state had risen to 219. Swett traveled the state pleading the case for the creation of more public schools. Coming from Massachusetts roots and having attended schools influenced by the philosophy of Horace Mann, Swett openly discussed his efforts to create a similar system in California, even quoting Mann in some of his speeches. As such, there were still elements of the early New England and Americanization philosophies present in the state's policies regarding education. The Revised School Law of 1865, for example, states that

> It shall be the duty of teachers to endeavor to impress on the minds of their pupils the principles of morality, truth, justice, and patriotism; to teach them to avoid idleness, profanity, and falsehood; to instruct them in the principles of a free government, and to train them up to a true comprehension of the rights, duties, and dignity of American citizenship. (Swett, 1876, p. 52)

Finally, largely through Swett's efforts to finalize the earlier educators' efforts to create public schooling, Swett was able to orchestrate the final stages of the creation of a statewide public school system. For his efforts, he has been called the "Father of the Public School System of California." *(For a description of John Swett's vision for a free, public education system in California, check the website at the Virtual Museum of the City of San Francisco at http://www.sfmuseum.org/hist3/schools.html.)*

In the 1866–1867 school year, Superintendent Swett claimed that the dream of free, public education in California was successful. In his Second Biennial Report of 1866–1867, he wrote:

> For the first time in the history of the State, every public school was made entirely free for every child to enter . . . I am glad that in this, my last official report, I can say that a system of *free schools*, supported by taxation, is an accomplished fact . . . The average length

> of time during which public schools are maintained during the year is 7.2 months. Last year, for the first time in the history of the State, *all* the schools were kept *free* to all pupils for a period of from 3 to 5 months. (Swett, 1876, pp. 47–49)

Educational Segregation in California

Despite the claim that all children in California were able to attend free, public schools by 1867, in reality, early California leaders had tried to restrict public education to only White children. The California public school system was being developed amid local, state, and national histories of racial and national conflict. Having just come out of the Mexican-American War in 1848, the state was undergoing massive shifts in who held the political power within the state. Further, developing as the U.S. Civil War was in progress, California was not immune to the ideological passions regarding race that separated the country. As will be seen, California practiced exclusion early in its history, when separate schools were established for students of color. And although legal segregation ended for African-American children from the 1870s–1890s, 60 years before the U.S. Supreme Court declared segregation illegal in *Brown vs. Board of Education,* there has been a series of fits and starts regarding equal education for all races and national origins, corresponding with social issues in California throughout the last 150 years. In several cases, the Superintendents of Public Instruction who passionately argued for free, public schooling for "all children," at the same time actually helped establish the laws that kept children of color out of those very same schools. As the Superintendent of Public Instruction wrote in his *Second Annual Report* of 1858,

> Had it been intended by the framers of the law that the children of the inferior races should be educated side by side with the whites, it is manifest the census would have included children of all colors. If this attempt to force African, Chinese and Diggers [Native Americans] into our white schools is persisted in, it must result in the ruin of our schools. (As Andrew J. Moulder, Superintendent of Public Instruction, wrote in Ferrier, 1937, p. 98)

Educational Laws Regarding Racial Segregation

The first school law that specifically mentioned segregation was the School Law of 1855, Section 18. This law changed the way that schools received their funding, regulating that rather than getting funding for the total number of students attending a school, the funding of public schools was instead to be based only on the number of White children attending. Since schools would only receive funding for the White children in their schools once this law was enacted, schools only wanted to have White children attending the schools. Thus it became commonly accepted for schools to deny access to children of color.

However, this common practice of keeping the races segregated was not enough for the framers of the laws. A law was extended in 1860 to make this segregation more clearly obvious. This law stated that it was illegal to admit children of color—in this case "Negro and Mongolian"—in White schools, under penalty of losing all state funds. So what started as the implication that only Whites should attend the public schools became law by 1860.

The tone of the laws changed in 1866, allowing some recognition of the need to provide education for children of color within the various towns in the state. The Revised School Law of 1866, Section 57–59, stated that if there were 10 African or Chinese children in a town, and if their parents signed a petition to ask for education, then the state would provide funding for a separate school for the children. This was an interesting progression in that the legislators wanted to be able to provide education for children of color, but they did not want that education to occur within the schools where their own children attended.

The tone of the laws shifted a bit again in 1872, when the law stated that "The education of children of African descent and Indian children must be provided for in separate schools; provided, that if the directors or trustees fail to provide such separate schools, then such children must be admitted into the schools for white children." This provided just enough of a shift to allow communities to make their own decisions regarding whether to allow Black children, especially, to attend the regular school. As a result, in 1875 San Francisco abolished its separate schools for Blacks, with 75 students then being allowed to enter the White schools. This trend continued in other cities, and by 1880 the cities of Sacramento, Vallejo, and Oakland had also abolished their separate schools for Black children.

By 1880, Section 1662 of the state law stated that "schools must be open for the admission of all children" (Wollenberg, 1976, p. 25).

"Colored Schools" for Black Children

The first "colored school," a school for Black children, was opened in 1854 in San Francisco. This was early in the development of education in the state, as the first public school for Whites had opened in San Francisco, only in 1851. This shows the conflicting values of the people of the state at this time. While education was valued enough to provide public schools for White children and for Blacks and later Chinese in San Francisco, the people still did not want the children to mix racially. This was followed by openings of separate colored schools in various towns across the northern part of the state, including in Sacramento in 1856, Marysville in 1858, and Stockton in 1868. These colored schools were almost all opened in the basements or back rooms of the Black churches of the time, and the efforts of Black leaders and community members to gain public funding for the "colored schools" should be highlighted. Despite not having the right to speak publicly to testify in court, the Black communities undertook the challenge of speaking at city hall and town council meetings, proposing the idea that education should be a free and public right for Black children as well as White. Black communities organized three State Conventions of the Colored Citizens of California in the 1850s, coming together to prepare to advocate for educational and other rights. The statement written at the first Convention illustrates these efforts to gain public schools.

> As a class, the colored people have to a great extent been deprived of the advantages of education, the means and opportunities of intellectual culture . . . As parents and guardians, we are under the most solemn obligations to have our children educated; upon any other conditions, our hopes and expectations of the future are vain . . . When our characters, as a people, shall fully combine the elements of learning, sound morality, and wealth, we shall be free and respected by all. (Proceedings of the First State Convention of the Colored Citizens of California, 1855/rpt. 1969, 1st Convention Day, pp. 24–25)

Schools for Chinese Children

The first Asians to enter the United States in large numbers were from China. Passing through the West Coast's version of Ellis Island—Angel Island in the San Francisco Bay—male Chinese entered the United States originally as workers who intended to return to their families in China. Chinese immigrants were males of working age, and they found work mainly in the gold mines, in mining communities, and later as workers on the railroads, while others gained some middle-class status in San Francisco. After several decades of racial tensions around jobs and businesses, the U.S. Congress passed the Chinese Exclusion Act in 1882, the first to deny immigration rights to a specific race. In 1892, the Chinese Exclusion Act was renewed for another 10 years, and when that 10 years was up, the act was renewed indefinitely. It was not until 1943, following World War II, that the United States "rewarded" China for its work as an ally by allowing a mere 100 immigrants per year to enter the United States.

Educational law for Chinese children in early California followed the same pattern as that for Black children (see earlier in the chapter). Both were excluded from public schools. However, even though the exclusionary language for Blacks and Chinese was removed in 1880, schools still practiced segregation of Chinese children. By the early 1880s, there were 75,000 Chinese residents in California, including over 700 children in the Chinatown section of San Francisco (Wollenberg, 1976). While the majority of Chinese had come to California as laborers in the mines and later to build the railroads, San Francisco was also the main location for merchants and social and economic associations. Chinese culture was celebrated, with a Cantonese opera company opening in 1852 and the first Chinese-language newspaper in 1854. Despite these economic and social gains, Chinese children were still being excluded from public schools.

In 1857, a group of Chinese families in San Francisco asked the Board of Education to provide a school for their children, since law did not allow the children to attend the regular public schools. The first school for Chinese children was indeed opened in 1859. Following the pattern of the Colored Schools, it opened in the basement of a church. However, it was not well attended, so in 1860, the Board of Education reorganized it as a night school to be able to help Chinese workers learn English. Following more anti-Chinese sentiment, the school closed in 1871.

In its place came a series of missionary schools. By 1871, there were English-language schools provided by Presbyterians, Baptists, Methodists, and Episcopalians (Wollenberg, 1976). Enrollment was reported to be 5,500 students—children and adults—but attendance was closer to 2,000. As with the Spanish Missions that inculcated Native Americans into the Christian way of life and beliefs, the missionary schools also used Americanization and Christianization practices along with their instruction in English.

But these were not free public schools offering an academic curriculum. In efforts to receive a free and public education, various petitions were sent to the San Francisco School Board in the 1870s, all of which failed to receive enough support to open schools for the Chinese children. In 1884, a school for Chinese children was opened in San Francisco in order to keep the Chinese children from entering the all-White schools. Finally, in 1905, San Francisco allowed Chinese children to enter the public schools, although the separate schools continued, and one had over 700 students by 1920.

Schools for Native American Children

No discussion of Native Americans in California can be truthful without laying out the significant impact of the Mission system. In just 50 years of the existence of the missions (1769–1821), over 100,000 California Native Americans died from illnesses such as diphtheria, measles, and pneumonia; malnutrition and wars/battles were other causes of death. In addition to loss of life, native cultures were purposefully diminished and distinguished through forced indoctrination into the United States by many federal and California policies, as well as by the California missions, and later by the public schools. The impact of the 26 missions, built by Native American labor, on loss of Native culture and life cannot be overstated. As Dutchke (2014) describes:

> Spain's Indian policy at the time of the invasion of California was a mixture of economic, military, political, and religious motives. Indians were regarded by the Spanish government as subjects of the Crown and human beings capable of receiving the sacraments of Christianity... It was essential under "missionization" that California Indians be "reduced" into settled and stable communities where they would become good subjects of the King and children of God. (p. 3)

This fervent belief that California's Native Americans needed to be inculcated into Christianity was echoed in the United States and California's treatment of Native Americans through the educational system. Barred from receiving a free public education by legislation that banned "diggers" from schools (as previously mentioned), Native American education fell to outsiders, especially missionaries, and enforced a strong Americanization and Christianization focus. These beliefs were also fortified by the national "civilization" philosophies. The language of civilized is interspersed with "savages" consistently throughout the educational philosophy and policy at the time. While not directly connected, the United States in 1819 established the "Civilization Fund Act," setting aside funding to establish schools for Native Americans "for introducing among them the habits and arts of civilization." As the Indian Affairs Commissioner in 1902 remarked, the U.S. government developed a policy to deal "with wild bands of marauding savages... It was a matter of segregating and confining them ... upon limited areas, where they could either be under definite surveillance or exterminated as a race" (*Annual Reports*, 1902, pp. 9–10). This language sets the tone for the purposes of educating Native American children from the 1820s to the 1930s, which set about "civilizing," "Americanizing," "Christianizing," and removing culture from Native Americans (Noel, 2002).

In California, three types of educational systems were established for Native Americans, all provided by those sharing the philosophies described earlier. First, the federal government established schools on the reservations. Second, the federal government established boarding schools, which removed children from their home communities, often with no rights to return. And third, they were being allowed to attend public schools (Heizer, 1978). While the public schools seemed the best alternative, most Indians did not have the right to attend these schools until the 1920s. Noel (2002) lays out the time frames and purposes of these different types of schools for Native Americans (*see Table 1.3*).

TABLE 1.3 - EDUCATION OF NATIVE AMERICANS

Years	Type of Schools	Purposes
1820s–1870s	Missionary schools	"Christianizing"
1870s–1900s	Off-reservation boarding schools	"Indoctrinating"
1900s–1910s	On-reservation boarding schools	"Civilizing"
1920+	Public schools	"Assimilating"

Note: Adapted from Noel, 2002, p. 20.

Equity and Social Justice Issues

There are a host of equity and social justice issues for all children in the history of California education. All groups, especially based on race, ethnic, or economic status, dealt with prejudice and discrimination as California was establishing its educational system. For further information on education of diverse California students, see Chapter Six: Immigration and Language Policies in California, which will address education for Mexican and Mexican-American children as well as for Japanese children.

Reflective and Action-Based Questions

1. *Observe in a classroom and your school for one day to determine which practices are being undertaken for either the explicit or subtle purpose of Americanization of students. Create a list of Americanization activities that you have observed. Discuss your beliefs about the appropriateness or inappropriateness of these practices.*
2. *Select one racial or ethnic group discussed in this chapter and trace their efforts to gain access to free public schooling in California.*
3. *Discuss three impacts the Gold Rush had on the development of education in California.*
4. *Identify and describe one piece of information you learned about California from this chapter that surprised you.*

References

Annual Reports of the Department of the Interior. (1902). Report of the Commissioner, Indian Affairs. Washington, DC: Government Printing Office.

Dutschke, D. (2014, October). A history of American Indians in California: Introduction. *Five views: An ethnic historic site survey for California.* Retrieved from http://ohp.parks.ca.gov/pages/1054/files/american%20indians%20in%20california.pdf

Ferrier, W. W. (1937). *Ninety years of education in California, 1846–1936: A presentation of educational movements and their outcome on education today.* Berkeley: Sather Gate Book Shop.

Heizer, R. F. (1978). *Handbook of North American Indians, Vol. 8: California.* Washington, DC: Smithsonian Institution.

Hendrick, I. G. (2000). From indifference to imperative duty: Educating children in early California. *California History, 79*(2), 226–249.

Noel, J. (2002). Education toward cultural shame: A century of Native American education. *Educational Foundations, 16*(1), 19–32.

Proceedings of the First State Convention of the Colored Citizens of the State of California. (1855). In Adam S. Eterovich (Ed.), *Proceedings of the First State Convention of the Colored Citizens of the State of California, 1855*, rpt. 1969. San Francisco: R & E Research Associates, Inc.

Swett, J. (1876). *History of the public school system in California.* San Francisco: A. L. Bancroft.

Wollenberg, C. (1976). *All deliberate speed: Segregation and exclusion in California schools, 1855–1975.* Berkeley: University of California Press.

CHAPTER TWO

Political Influences and Organizational Structure of Education In California

Guiding Questions

1. *What are the roles of the U.S. Department of Education and the California Department of Education in K-12 education?*
2. *What are the most recent national educational trends, and what has been California's responses?*
3. *What are two paths for an idea to move from initial point to state law?*

Introduction

K-12 EDUCATION IN the United States is based on an intricate balance between national policy, state-level efforts, and local contexts, as well as between racial and economic equity and international competition. Educational policy changes according to shifting social, cultural, and economic contexts over time and reflects the concerns of the nation and of communities in its evolving nature. Added to this complexity is that the policy-making process allows voters to vote on bills that would change or add new educational policy and that federal and state lawsuits can result in change to educational law. Within this complexity, several levels of organizational structure help to organize the K-12 educational system. This chapter presents two focal points: the influence of U.S. and state politics on education, and the way that K-12 education is structured within California. The chapter also includes a discussion of the ways that educators and communities can be involved in the political process surrounding education.

National Education Politics and Policies

U.S. Department of Education

The U.S. Department of Education (DOE) is the nation's agency entrusted with setting educational policy and supporting K-12 and higher education throughout the nation. It was founded in 1867 to help gather and pass on information to the states. Over time, several different federal agencies held responsibility for different pieces of the nation's educational system, including the Department of the Interior and the Department of Health and Human Services. In 1980, all of these efforts were combined to create the current U.S. Department of Education.

It is not the role of the DOE to fund the actual functioning schools, and currently it funds approximately 8% of all K-12 education in the United States. The DOE sets the budget and priorities of what schools will need to address each year and provides information to legislators for the purposes of passing education laws. Its mission is "to promote student achievement and preparation for global competitiveness by fostering educational excellence and ensuring equal access." However, this has not always been the mission of the DOE, largely because the U.S. Secretary of Education is appointed by the president and then approved by Congress. Secretaries of education, then, feel the responsibility to put into place the priorities of the political administration. Further, secretaries of education tend to be replaced with each new incoming president, meaning that the focus of educational policies and priorities shifts to match the social and political beliefs of each new president. For example, the mission of the DOE in 1997 was "to ensure equal access to education and to promote educational excellence throughout the nation." The differences in missions in these time periods point to the differences in political climate within the country. California mirrors these shifting priorities. These national and state reform movements will be discussed in the following section.

National Reform Movements and California's Responses

In the changing mission statement of the U.S. Department of Education over time, we see the two main, and sometimes competing, directions of education in the United States: equity and global competitiveness. It is these two directions that have guided educational movements since the 1960s. Most changes can be seen as attempts to reconcile efforts at achieving racial and economic equity with efforts to maintain the nation's international competitiveness, or as commonly stated today, between equity and accountability. Several educational researchers lay the framework within which education has been formed since the 1960s as "fear of failing" (Krejsler, 2018) or a "sense of losing" (Ravitch, 2013). These are concerns that have driven changes in educational policy and practice over the past 50 years.

Elementary and Secondary Education Act (ESEA), 1965

Prior to 1965, K-12 education throughout the United States was controlled primarily by local school districts. As can be imagined, there was tremendous variation across communities, states, and regions regarding what should be the priorities of a K-12 education. Skrla and Scheurich's 2004 observation would have described the situation well: "it is as if there are 50 somewhat different games going on at one time. The components of each game differ from those of the other games" (p. 19). The Elementary and Secondary Act (ESEA) has served as the basis for education since 1965, and Congress must reauthorize it every six years, often with significant revisions.

In the 1960s, the country was in the midst of a Civil Rights movement that was to change the nation. New federal programs were put into place to assist those living in poverty and those who did not receive equitable treatment in the country. (It is debatable whether lives have improved in recent times.) In education, it was considered that the nation would need to step in to assist, especially in those states and school districts around the country where people were suffering the most from racial and economic inequality. Against this backdrop, the United States passed the ESEA in 1965, with the hopes of raising opportunities through improved education. With the ESEA came funding for Local Education Agencies (LEAs, commonly known as school districts) that served areas of high numbers of children from low-income families. The hope was to close the "achievement gap," language which now includes "opportunity gap," between the privileged and underprivileged racial and socioeconomic groups.

While ESEA may seem like a noble attempt to provide better education for all students in the United States, in reality it also was a strong expression of the "fear of failing" that is at the heart of the accountability movement. The cause for concern? Sputnik. In 1957, at a time when global superpowers were flexing their scientific and military muscles, Russia launched Sputnik, the first satellite to be able to transmit information around the world. This triggered what is known as the "space race" and drew the United States and Russia into the Cold War. How was the United States to react? A key response was to create a stronger science and math focus in schools, for the purpose of ensuring that "talent" be identified and brought into the service of the United States in its competition with Russia.

California's response. California was one of the first three states to enact a statewide assessment program in the 1960s. (The others were New York and Pennsylvania.) While the assessment system has changed and been revised over time, it began as a response to the equity and accountability requirements of ESEA of 1965.

A Nation at Risk Report, 1983

In 1983, the National Commission of Excellence in Education released an influential report that would shift the federal focus in education even more toward alleviating the "fear of failing" and encouraging global competitiveness. *A Nation at Risk: The Imperative for Educational Reform* reported that even with the changes initiated as result of the Sputnik scare and the ESEA, the nation's students were still falling behind other nations in measures such as SAT scores. Of particular concern was that students from Japan and Germany were scoring at a higher level than students from the United States. (This fear is still voiced today in the context of the United States' losing its dominance in the world based on lower student test scores.) To avert this seeming decline, the language of educational reform and accountability took on a more urgent tone. Standardized testing, in which all students take identical tests and then are measured on their test scores, became a priority that dominates even today. (See Chapter Five for further discussion.) The hope was that by requiring all students, either in a particular state or across the nation (the latter being the current trend), to take the same tests to measure their knowledge about the same information, schools could then use that information to improve education for those who scored at a lower level. However, this standardized testing also became a tool for enacting punishing consequences for schools with lower test scores.

California's response. The period following the *A Nation at Risk* report was a tumultuous one for both the nation's education system and that of California. As Timar (2003) describes the 1980s and 1990s: "For the past two decades, the legislature has routinely enacted during each session literally hundreds of measures dealing with K-12 education" (p. 188). The state, districts, and schools had to create ways of dealing with these new and often shifting requirements. Of particular significance was the 1999 Public Schools Accountability Act (PSAA), which was designed to align California with the national movement toward accountability in ensuring that each child make progress in academic achievement. PSAA had a primary focus on developing a way to measure schools' progress in helping their students achieve academic success. To that end, the CDE created the Academic Performance Index (API) (discussed further in Chapter Five: Assessment and Accountability Practices and Issues). The API was developed to provide a way to measure the advancement of a school's students toward predetermined test score targets. Test scores were made public in the hope that this would improve school accountability. PSAA also provided a mechanism for funding high-achieving schools and programs, as well as for penalizing schools with lower test scores (see Chapter Six for further discussion). All of these were designed to address the equity and accountability climate that had been developing for 20 years in the United States, and were a precursor to the No Child Left Behind Act of 2001.

No Child Left Behind Act of 2001 (NCLB), signed in 2002

NCLB became the most highly focused effort on behalf of standardized testing. Almost everything in schools became related to students' achieving high test scores, leading to the term "high-stakes testing." The NCLB has as its stated purpose "to close the achievement gap with accountability, flexibility, and choice, so that no child is left behind." While the text of NCLB is lengthy, the three points that have had the biggest impact on schools are (a) "improving the academic achievement of the disadvantaged"; (b) "preparing, training, and recruiting high quality teachers and principals"; and (c) "promoting informed parental choice and innovative programs." Each of these has the purpose ensuring that all students receive a quality education, and if they don't, their parents should have the choice to move their children to a different school. (See more about the "school choice" movement later in this chapter.) There was an almost universal response among states that to measure improved academic achievement, there would need to be a greater focus on testing. Funding formulas at the federal and state levels then became dependent on whether or not the "lowest performing" schools, those with the most disadvantaged children and lowest test scores, improved their test scores. (See Chapter Six for further discussion.) When low-income schools failed to show increased test scores in 20 states, those states (including California) imposed punishments on those schools, including the firing of all teachers or being taken over by the state.

The intent was that a market-driven educational system, one in which schools must show a prescribed set of results or risk losing students to higher-achieving schools, would ensure an increase in the quality of all schools. While sounding noble in its intent, the focus on test scores led to harsh criticism from educators, who pointed out that socioeconomic factors, especially poverty, impact test scores, and that punishing schools for not achieving high test scores is equivalent to punishing students for being underprivileged. (Critics, especially from that time frame, include Dorn, 2007; Kantor & Lowe, 2006; Meier & Wood, 2004; Ogawa & Collom, 2000; Ravitch, 2013; and Timar, 2003, among many others.) Other criticisms are that such a law shifts decisions about education from the local to the national level. An equally concerning point raised by a number of educators is the move toward using educational funds to pay the corporations who create and administer the newly developed tests. In California's case, in 2015 the state signed a $240 million, 3-year contract with Educational Testing Service (ETS) to administer the state's K-12 standardized tests. The U.S. Department of Education summarizes what it sees as the outcome of NCLB, which is that it "shined a light on where students were making progress and where they needed additional support, regardless of race, income, zip code, disability, home language, or background" (https://www.ed.gov/ESSA).

While the focus on equity is seen in the title and the purpose, that no child should be left behind by the educational system, the longest-lasting legacy of NCLB is its sharp directive to focus on accountability, which has been interpreted as "high-stakes testing." Most critics have recognized the clear focus on accountability more than on equity. As Kantor and Lowe (2006) explain:

> But the emphasis in recent federal legislation is not principally on the distribution of dollars to schools with large numbers of low-income students. In response to the failure of compensatory federal spending

> to make a significant impact on achievement, it has shifted instead to accountability—to making certain that schools use federal funds efficiently by requiring states to set performance standards for students, monitoring schools to make sure that they meet these standards, and sanctioning them if they do not. (p. 480)

One of the impacts of NCLB was that schools were now required to let parents know if the school did not meet its annual test score targets. The notification to parents would additionally offer them the option to move their child to a different public school that had higher test scores. This was an early indication of what is now called the "school choice" movement, discussed later in this chapter.

California's response. Since California had already been judging school performance based on student scores for several decades, the state spent the time following NCLB honing its systems. In particular, each school must now develop a School Accountability Report Card (SARC), which is posted publicly on various state, district, and school-level websites. Included in the SARC is demographic information, test scores by grade and subject matter, descriptions of the curriculum used, qualifications of teachers, and many additional descriptors of the schools. The SARC is intended to make public—for parents, community members, and legislators—the quality of a school based on these various indicators. The belief is that the public nature of such data will lead to school improvements.

Every Student Succeeds Act, 2015

The latest reauthorization of the ESEA came in 2015 with the Every Student Succeeds Act (ESSA). Because of the time it takes to make large-scale changes, the ESSA provisions did not go into effect until the 2017–2018 school year. ESSA made a number of changes to the ever-evolving ESEA, but the main summary is that it has moved a bit away from high-stakes testing and a bit more toward returning some decisions to the states, while still focusing on high-level standards and increased academic achievement. ESSA requires, among others:

- Accountability goals and plans. States can set their own goals, as long as the emphasis is on reducing the gap between achievement and graduation rates of privileged and underprivileged students.

- Increased focus on English Learners. Actually, the focus is on increased accountability related to English Learners, tying their test scores to overall school achievement.

- Teachers. The term "highly qualified" teachers, a cornerstone of NCLB, has been removed. New resources are provided to offer teachers additional professional development, especially in the areas of literacy and STEM.

- "Challenging" standards. Each state must adopt what the U.S. Department of Education calls challenging standards. While no single set of standards is proscribed, 45 states, including California, have now adopted the Common Core standards (see below and Chapter Four for further description).

- States can select standards. In a change from NCLB, states may now include additional components of the education system to include within their reporting of whether standards are met. Some have suggested that this may include factors such as student engagement in the classroom, school safety, and overall school climate.

California's response. California elected to institute two large-scale revisions in response to ESSA: Common Core (see more in Chapter Four) and Smarter Balanced Assessment (see Chapter Six). These are both available nationwide and were created jointly by teachers, higher education faculty, and educational testing experts.

The Common Core State Standards ("Common Core") in English Language Arts/Literacy and Mathematics were established to better prepare K-12 students for college and careers. Led by the Council of Chief State School Officers and the National Governors Association, the development of Common Core involved educational leaders, administrators, teachers, and the governors from 48 states, making it a wide-ranging and immensely impactful set of standards. With 45 states currently having adopted Common Core, students can be more assured that if they were to move to different districts or even into other states, the standards for academic achievement would be roughly the same (see Chapter Four for a more detailed description of Common Core).

The Smarter Balanced Assessment System uses computerized tests, as well as tasks that ask students to perform their knowledge ("performance based tests"), with the purpose of ensuring that all students have the opportunity to demonstrate their understanding of the Common Core curriculum. Importantly, it is designed so that it is accessible to all students, including students with disabilities, whose knowledge is often minimized simply by the structure of the tests.

School Choice and Privatization

A growing movement in the past decade has been "school choice," which proponents believe will provide a market-based improvement to all schools. In other words, if parents have the choice of sending their children to any public (or, as some propose, private) school, they will pull out of underperforming schools and move to higher-performing schools. With the push for school choice, charter schools and vouchers are often part of the discussion.

Charter schools are public schools, receiving funding from state funds, with some located within school districts and others being operated independently. Charter schools are often, but not always, initiated by local communities that want to see a better school for their children. Charter schools have greater flexibility in hiring, curriculum decisions, and management, with most having self-appointed school boards that serve only the school. Proponents believe that this flexibility gives schools more independence to develop more innovative programs. Some charter schools are not run by the community, though, as there are national chains that operate networks of charter schools across multiple states, including Aspire and KIPP (Knowledge Is Power Program).

Vouchers have been proposed by a number of states, and discussed at the national level, as a way to help parents move their children from low-performing schools to higher performing schools that are located farther from their homes. With this change in schools often comes a need for transportation, or a need to pay new fees for activities. Vouchers are set amounts of money that parents can use to cover these costs. Critics are concerned that some conversations about vouchers advocate for the use of publicly funded vouchers to pay for private school tuition, thus blurring the line between public and private.

Opponents raise a host of concerns, pointing out that in California, for instance, schools do not need to report test scores publicly and teachers do not have to have teaching credentials. Another critical concern of educators is that the school choice movement is driven by corporate interests (Ravitch, 2013). It matters who serves on state boards of education, or who is elected State Superintendent of Public Instruction, as these positions determine the direction of education in states. Funding makes a difference in these elections, as funding can pay for TV and internet ads that reach a wide audience. Ravitch (2013) illustrates the role played by wealthy business operators ("philanthropists") or heads of corporations in funding both the elections of people across the country running on pro-privatization or school choice agendas, or for voter approval of pro-charter school initiatives. Key funders of these election campaigns included Eli Broad (the Broad Foundation), Michael Bloomberg (Bloomberg), the Walton family (Walmart), Bill Gates (Microsoft), the Bezos family (Amazon), Rupert Murdoch (Fox News), and Michelle Rhee (StudentsFirst). While many individuals in each location also contributed to these funds, the influx of funding from multinational corporations for the purpose of affecting local or state elections effectively serve to push forward the school-choice agenda (*see Figure 2.1*).

FIGURE 2.1 - EXAMPLES OF SPENDING ON SCHOOL CHOICE EFFORTS

- Louisiana—In 2011, donors spent $2.6 million to elect a proponent of privatization to the state board of education. This was 34 times the money spent on the election campaign by the candidate who supported traditional public schools.
- Washington—An initiative to allow for the opening of charter schools in the state was rejected three times previously by voters. However, in 2012, funding from Bill Gates, the Walton family, and the Bezos family provided $11 million to support the initiative, which passed in 2012.
- Nationally—Michelle Rhee, a longtime advocate of school reform, provided support through her organization Students First to 105 candidates nationwide who supported vouchers and the overriding of local school district boards.

Note: Adapted from Ravitch, 2013

With this support of some of the wealthiest people in the United States, critics are concerned that the school choice agenda will be moved forward, simply due to the influence of wealth.

California's response. In actuality, what has been described in this chapter as "California's response" is often "California's contributions" to the educational trend. Such is the case with the school choice trend. California was the second state to pass a law approving charter schools, in 1992. Today, 630,000 students attend 1,275 charter schools, more students and schools than any other state. In 2013, Los Angeles had more charter schools than any other city in the nation.

How do state funding and corporate donations interact with charter schools? The roadmap to following a charter school's funding is not simple. As public schools, they receive funding from the state in the same way that traditional public schools are funded (see Chapter Three). The concern for many educators is that a number of these charter schools are part of national chains, run by for-profit corporations. The leading charter school corporation in California is K12 Inc., which received $310 million from the state of California for operating its 16 schools over the past decade, through a largely online program. California's funding contributed to the company's 2016 revenue of $872 million, including $89 million paid to its Wall Street investors.

To correct this practice of making a profit off of K-12 schools, in 2015, California put an end to the operation of charter schools by for-profit organizations through passage of bill AB-787. However, these companies still operated a number of charter schools, so another attempt to end this practice was signed into law by the governor in 2018, bill AB-406. This bill prohibits charter schools from being operated by "a for-profit corporation, a for-profit educational management organization, or a for-profit charter management organization." So while California was an early proponent of charter schools, and has the most children attending charter schools, it is making an effort to ensure that state funding does not go to support for-profit corporations and their commonly supportive Wall Street investors.

Organizational Structure, Politics, and Policies of K-12 Education in California

California's public school system follows regulations set out by the federal government and receives funding from the feds for various programs, but it is organized at the state and local levels. The main structural components of education at the state level are the California Department of Education, the State Superintendent of Public Instruction, and the State Board of Education. Each has specific roles, but they work together to administer education at the state level.

California Department of Education (CDE)

The CDE was established by law in 1921 as a way to deal with a growing population that needed a better way to manage the increasing number of students and schools. The CDE also provided a structure to deal with both state and national issues such as World War I. The CDE is the overall umbrella structure within which everything related to statewide policy, data, funding, and resources is managed. It is the role of CDE to ensure that the educational system statewide is operating effectively to best educate all children.

CDE describes its "Beliefs and Purposes" in the following way. (*See Figure 2.2 on page 27 for the list of CDE "Roles and Responsibilities."*)

> California will provide a world-class education for all students, from early childhood to adulthood. The Department of Education serves our state by innovating and collaborating with educators, schools, parents, and community partners. Together, as a team, we prepare students to live, work, and thrive in a multicultural, multilingual, and highly connected world.

Within the CDE, the State Board of Education (SBE) is the actual policy-making unit. It has 11 members, all appointed by the state's governor, but includes teachers and other educators, one student, and one member from the state legislature. The SBE takes the propositions and bills passed by the state and turns them into policy for academic standards, curriculum, instructional materials, assessments, and accountability.

FIGURE 2.2 - CALIFORNIA DEPARTMENT OF EDUCATION ROLES AND RESPONSIBILITIES

- Holding local educational agencies accountable for student achievement in all programs and for all groups of students
- Building local capacity to enable all students to achieve state standards
- Expanding and improving a system of recruiting, developing, and supporting teachers that instills excellence in every classroom— preschool through adult
- Providing statewide leadership that promotes the effective use of technology to improve teaching and learning
- Increasing efficiency and effectiveness in administration of kindergarten through grade twelve education, including student record keeping, and good financial management practices
- Providing broader and more effective communication among the home, school, district, county, and state
- Establishing and fostering systems of school, home, and community resources that provide the physical, emotional, and intellectual support that each student needs to succeed
- Advocating for additional resources and flexibility, and providing statewide leadership that promotes good business practices so that California schools can target their resources to ensure success for all students
- Improving the effectiveness and efficiency of the Department

Note: CDE Roles and Responsibilities listed on the CDE website at https://www.cde.ca.gov/eo/mn/rr

The position of California Superintendent of Public Instruction was established within the state's Constitution (Article IX, Section 1). The superintendent is elected every four years by the state's voting population, is Executive Director of the California Department of Education, and serves on the State Board of Education. As such, the superintendent directs the functioning of the CDE and ensures that it meets all of its roles in improving the state's education system. The superintendent is also a spokesperson for education throughout California.

In summary, the CDE, State Board of Education, and State Superintendent of Public Instruction are responsible for enforcing education law and regulations and for continuing to reform and improve public K-12 education.

Education Code

California's education system (including K-12, community colleges, and higher education) is regulated by the "Education Code," a very large and ever-evolving set of over 100,000 laws regulating schools. (See Appendix A for further details on the Education Code.) All state laws for education are contained within the Education Code (EdCode). As can be imagined, this is a very lengthy document, and grows increasingly lengthy with each new policy created. The website http://leginfo.legislature.ca.gov/faces/codesTOCSelected.xhtml?tocCode=EDC provides a way to search the EdCode for any laws of particular interest. While the language has legal tones, in order for each policy to meet the requirements of state or federal law, reviewing the EdCode is a very good way to learn about the thousands of laws that govern education in California.

Making Educational Policy in California

Making educational policy is generally a lengthy process, with opportunities for input from educators and the public-at-large. One method is through the proposal of a legislative bill, designated as SB (Senate Bill) or AB (Assembly Bill). In these cases, a state senator or assembly member can propose a bill to change or introduce new educational policy. When policy is initiated in this way, there is a formal time period for the public to provide input, several readings by the legislature, approval by both the Senate and the House, and eventual signature by the governor. Once the SB or AB has been approved and signed, then comes the work of getting the new language inserted into the EdCode. This can sometimes take a year or more to go through all of these steps. So we can rest assured that educational policy is not made hastily.

Sometimes California education policy begins as a proposition, put forward on a ballot for residents to vote on in an election. Californians can vote on what they want to see in education through the proposition process. As with legislative bills, once passed, the propositions must then be put into the language needed to add it to the EdCode.

Finally, education policy is sometimes generated from a lawsuit challenging a certain part of the education system. As in other types of lawsuits, ones related to education often go to trial, where people can make their statements, experts can be called upon to provide evidence (these are often college professors), and lawyers can make their arguments. If the outcome is a ruling that a policy must change, or that a new policy must be developed, then the State Board of Education once again turns that into policy language for the EdCode.

One Example—Special Education from Federal to State Law

To illustrate how an educational policy that has been enacted at the federal level ends up in the California state educational policy, we can trace the special education policy known as IDEA (Individuals with Disabilities [improvement] Act) from its most recent reauthorization through to California state law. IDEA provides regulations to ensure that schools identify, locate, evaluate, and provide a means of educating children with identified disabilities. It requires that children with disabilities receive (a) a free and appropriate education, determined by school personnel with the parents of the child; (b) evaluation, or diagnosis, of the child's disability; (c) informed parent consent to the child's education plan, created by the Individualized Education Plan; (d) education in the least restrictive environment, meaning as much in the regular classroom as possible based on disability; (e) other regulations such as due process for the child and parents if there is a disagreement about the child's education.

- 2004–IDEA was formalized by Public Law 108-446, passed by Congress and signed into law by the president.
- 2005–provisions of the law to go into effect nationally on July 1, 2005.
- 2005–State Assembly Bill 1662 was passed and signed by the governor, to make changes in Education Code to be consistent with the reauthorized IDEA.
- 2005-present–As IDEA is revised with amendments, California responds by ensuring that the Education Code meets the requirements of federal law. Currently, Education Code 56000-56865 lays out California regulations for educating children with disabilities.

Issues of Equity and Social Justice

Issues of equity and social justice are evident throughout any discussion of the political influences on education. Most concerns relate to questions of power and privilege. Who makes the decisions impacting education, and who is left out of the decision-making process? Why does education still favor the privileged and diminish the underrepresented? The following reflective and action-based questions will ask you to consider these questions, based on the reading here and/or on your own experiences.

Reflective and Action-Based Questions

1. *Review the Education Code. Select three provisions that you believe are the most important to K-12 schools today, with a description of why you believe they are the most important.*
2. *Given that the U.S. Secretary of Education is appointed by each new incoming president, discuss how that impacts the direction of K-12 education with each new president.*
3. *The CDE lays out its statement of "beliefs and purpose." Write what you believe should be the "beliefs and purpose" of education in California.*

References

Dorn, S. (2007). *Accountability Frankenstein: Understanding and taming the monster.* Charlotte, NC: Information Age Publishing.

Every Student Succeeds Act. (2015). Washington, DC: U.S. Department of Education.

Gardner, D., and Others. (1983). *A nation at risk: The imperative for educational reform.* Washington, DC: The National Commission on Excellence in Education.

Kantor, H., & Lowe, R. (2006). From New Deal to no deal: No Child Left Behind and the devolution of responsibility for equal opportunity. *Harvard Educational Review, 76*(4), 474–502.

Krejsler, J. B. (2018). The "fear of falling behind regime" embraces school policy: State vs federal policy struggles in California and Texas. *International Journal of Qualitative Studies in Education, 31*(5), 393–408.

Meier, D., & Wood, G. (2004). *Many children left behind: How the No Child Left Behind Act is damaging our children and our schools.* Boston: Beacon Press.

No Child Left Behind Act. (2011). Washington, DC: U.S. Department of Education.

Ogawa, R. T., & Collom, E. (2000). Using performance indicators to hold schools accountable: Implicit assumptions and inherent tensions. *Peabody Journal of Education, 75*(4), 200–215.

Ravitch, D. (2013). *Reign of error: The hoax of the privatization movement and the danger to America's public schools.* New York: Alfred A. Knopf.

Skrla, L., & Scheurich, J. J. (2004). Thinking carefully about equity and accountability. In L. Skrla & J. J. Scheurich (Eds.), *Educational equity and accountability: Paradigms, policies, and politics* (pp. 13–29). New York: Routledge Falmer.

Timar, T. B. (2003). The "new accountability" and school governance in California. *Peabody Journal of Education, 78*(4), 177–200.

CHAPTER THREE

FUNDING EDUCATION IN CALIFORNIA

Guiding Questions

1. *From what sources does California receive its funding for education?*
2. *What are the trends in education funding related to local versus state funding?*

Introduction

SIMILAR TO THE rest of the country, California has long struggled with how to adequately fund its schools. According to a report from the U.S. Department of Education, over 40% of low-income schools nationally do not receive equal funding compared to schools with middle- to higher-income students (U.S. Department of Education, 2011). California has enacted a number of different strategies to pay for schools with public monies, with the result being a basic level of funding for all public schools. But many inequities exist across the state. A recent analysis of funding, from 2015, documents that California, once a leader in educational support, is 13% lower than the rest of the nation for per-pupil funding (Murphy & Paluch, 2018), ranking it 41st in the nation (Kaplan, 2017). This chapter will lay out the methods for paying for California's schools, including the funding formula, the system of categoricals, the Local Control Funding Formula (LCFF), and other special funding issues. Several court cases and propositions will be emphasized in particular that had major impacts on the schools. The focus will be on how the funding formulas over time have impacted students of different racial, national, linguistic, needs levels, and income levels.

Funding Sources

Funding for California's public schools comes largely from taxes, is based on attendance, and comes from several sources, including federal, state, and local funding, and even includes money from the California Lottery. Let's examine each of these further and then take a look at how this funding formula leads to wide discrepancies in amount of funding for districts throughout the state, and what has been started recently to try to provide more equitable funding (Murphy & Paluch, 2018). (*See Table 3.1 for a list and description of the sources of education funding in California.*)

Table 3.1 - California Education Funding Sources

Source of Funding	Percent of Total Funding	Further Details
State general funds	58%	Due to the passage of Proposition 98, the state must spend 40% of its state funds on K-14 education, which includes K-12 and community colleges.
Local property taxes	22%	Several court cases and propositions over the last 50 years have impacted the level of school funding that can come from local property taxes.
Other local funds	10%	Includes such items as local donations, interest on invested income, and leases on any unused property, among other sources.
Federal funds	9%	Funding designated for specific programs, especially related to education for lower income students. Usually comes in the form of grant funding.
State lottery	1%	Voters approved that 1% of state lottery funds would go to help fund California's schools, including K-14 and higher education.

Court Cases and Propositions Setting School Funding Levels

Until the 1970s, K-12 education in California was funded in a patchwork fashion, arranged by local districts and funded by local property taxes. If we consider the wide economic variation of property values in cities and towns across the state, it is easy to recognize that the funding varied widely from district to district. For example, in 1968–1969, the Beverly Hills Unified School District spent $1,231.72 per student per year, while the Baldwin Park Unified School District spent $577.49 per student per year (Durbin, 1972). This difference is despite the fact that Beverly Hills and Baldwin Hills are only six miles apart within the Los Angeles basin. With this recognition of the inequities that resulted from this inequitable funding, thus began a series of lawsuits, which continue to today, to try to provide greater equity in the funding of K-12 schools.

Serrano v Priest, 1971

In the court case *Serrano v Priest,* the family of student John Serrano and other Los Angeles area families filed a lawsuit against the California State Treasurer Ivy Baker Priest in 1968. Their claim was that the inequities in school funding, which are inequitable based solely on the wealth of a community, went against the Equal Protection Clause of the 14th Amendment to the U.S. Constitution. After several years of pursuing the case, The California Supreme Court in 1971 ruled in favor of the families, claiming that "the public school financing system which allows such a disparity in educational disbursements invidiously discriminates against the poor because it makes the quality of a child's education a function of the wealth of his parents and neighbors" (Durbin, 1972, p. 162). The outcome of this case was that California put a limit, or cap, on the amount of funding a district can utilize from property taxes to fund its schools, thus attempting to bring each district to equitable funding.

Proposition 13 ("Prop 13"), 1978

Prop 13 was passed by a large majority of voters in 1978 (64.8% voted in favor of the proposition) as a tax-reform initiative, and it still stands today, to the relief of some but to the consternation of many educators. Because the price of housing was rapidly increasing in the 1970s, Californians were concerned about quickly rising property taxes. Prop 13 changed the state tax law to stop the rising property taxes by restricting the property taxes to only 1% of the home's value, and limiting property taxes to grow only 2% per year. This meant that Californians were able to count on a more limited property tax system that would be quite stable over time. The result, however, was a dramatic reduction in local tax funding for K-12 education, lowering it by as much as 60% for some school districts. With this vote, the funding of schools, by necessity, moved toward educational funding provided by the state in order to make up for the drop in funding caused by Prop 13 and the mandate to fund schools more equitably.

Proposition 98 ("Prop 98"), 1988

By 1988, the educational system was not being funded at a level that would provide a quality education for California's children. With a growing student population and not enough facilities being built to provide education to the full population, California had become the state with the most overcrowded classrooms. Proposition 98—the Classroom Instructional Improvement and Accountability Act—was put to voters in 1988. They approved Prop 98 as a way to increase funding to K-12 schools, not by raising taxes, but rather by increasing to 40% the amount of state funds that would be used for the K-14 school system. This resulted in an increase in funding and a greater stability thereof.

Williams Case, 1997

With the ongoing struggles to provide equitable funding for all California students, conditions were still not equalizing for all students. In 1997, *Williams v California* was filed to try once more to equalize conditions (see more about the Williams case in Chapters Two and Six). Signed by the governor in 2004, the case brought to attention the severe inequities in availability of textbooks, qualified teachers, and clean and adequate facilities, based on race and socio-economic status. The findings included the following:

- Instructional materials. As described in Chapter Six, the findings regarding instructional materials were that "teachers working in schools with the highest concentrations of poor children were also most likely to have inadequate materials" (Oakes & Lipton, 2004, p. 241).
- Highly qualified teachers. In 1997, 45,000 teachers were teaching in California without teaching credentials, meaning they were not considered "highly qualified." However, these teachers were not evenly distributed throughout the state. Findings from the Los Angeles Unified School District presented at the Williams case trial were that "schools with fewer qualified teachers are disproportionately located in neighborhoods where most residents are Latino and African American" (Oakes & Lipton, 2004, p. 240).

- School facilities. While many school districts have schools that need repair, and infrastructure that needs to be updated, the Williams case pointed to a critical facility issue: overcrowding. In the most overcrowded schools, those with 150% of the number of students that the school was designed to hold, a new practice was created called "Concept 6." In the Concept 6 calendar, the school schedule was reduced by 17 days in order to squeeze in three separate schedules of children to be able to fit into the schools. This meant that students in Concept 6 schools attended school for nearly a month less than other students, with the attendant reduction in opportunities to learn the same material. In the Los Angeles School District, where almost all of the Concept 6 schools existed, "these schools have twice the percentage of Latino students as schools on regular calendars. All are located in low-income neighborhoods." (Oakes & Lipton, 2004, p. 242).

With this and other evidence provided, how did the Williams case end? What is the long term outcome? The judge indeed ruled that schools must be assisted in their efforts to move toward equality in these areas. As a result of the Williams case and settlement, every public school in California now is reviewed yearly for adherence to providing both enough and quality textbooks, hiring highly qualified teachers, and reducing overcrowding within school districts. Schools are reviewed each year and posted publicly in the School Accountability Report Cards. "Williams Uniform Complaint Procedures" have been made available to all districts and schools, to help keep track of these equity efforts. To facilitate these actions to bring schools into greater equity, California inserted into the Education Code 52055.770 that school district superintendents would receive funding to implement the required changes necessitated by the Williams case.

Proposition 30 ("Prop 30"), 2012

Following the trend over time of trying to provide a greater level of funding for K-14 schools, California's Prop 30 was proposed in 2012 as "Temporary Taxes to Fund Education." California voters passed Prop 30, voting to increase sales and state taxes specifically to fund education, even during a time when the United

States was in an anti-taxes mode. Sales taxes were raised from 7.25% to 7.5% for the entire state. State taxes were applied at different levels based on income levels. Individuals making less than $250,000 would have no state tax increase, with increasing taxes levied on those who make more money, with the greatest increase charged to those who make over $1 million. Followed by an extension applied to the taxes by Prop 55, this new tax formula will be in effect through 2030.

How California Spends Its Educational Funding

It costs a lot to operate K-12 education. Funding for K-12 schools in 2014–2015 was $45.3 billion from the California General Fund, with total funding from all state, local, and federal funds reaching $76.6 billion for the year. For those interested in "per-pupil funding," which is the amount of money spent per student, the average amount spent per pupil in California was $9,067. How is that funding spent? What does it take to provide education for schoolchildren? A thorough breakdown of financial data can be found for each school district at the website www.ed-data.org.

Types of Expenditures

The main types of expenditures are for instruction, but there are many other types of expenditures as well. Not every school or school district will utilize all types of expenditures, as they are used based on the needs of the students. (*An abbreviated list of school expenditures can be seen in Figure 3.1. on page 39.*)

Categoricals

In addition to the general funding that goes to schools and school districts, California's system of "categoricals" allowed schools to receive funding in 50 different categories, meant to provide funding for programs best designed to fit the needs of the local districts. This system has now been overridden by the Local Control Funding Formula (LCFF), described in the next section. Funding for categoricals was distributed based on an application format, often called grant funding for categoricals. These categoricals represented the areas of localized need for funding based on demographics within communities. Examples include American Indian Education Centers, Special Education transportation, and small

FIGURE 3.1 - EXAMPLES OF CALIFORNIA K-12 SCHOOL EXPENDITURES

- Instruction, mainly for teachers and instructional aides, including special education
- Instruction-related services such as curriculum development and libraries
- Pupil services, including but not limited to
    - Guidance and counseling
    - Health services
    - Speech pathology and audiology
    - Transportation
- Ancillary services, such as athletics and other extracurricular activities
- Community services, such as contributing to community recreation and other programs
- Administration
- Plant or facility maintenance

school district bus replacements. Because communities differ, not all 50 categoricals will be needed in each district, but they were available to supplement the funding of districts that had needs in these categories.

Local Control and LCFF

Despite 40 years of attempts to provide equitable funding for K-12 students across the state of California, school districts still received widely different levels of funding, still based on economic status, and correspondingly on race and cultural differences. As of 2013, school districts with widely different percentages of economically disadvantaged students received an inverse amount of funding, meaning that districts with larger percentages of economically disadvantaged students received less funding than wealthier districts (California Budget Project, 2013). To again address this change, the governor in 2013 set forth the Local Control Funding Formula (LCFF). This was a move to greater fund education, but it was also a recognition that local school districts should have greater control over how they spend their funding based on their local conditions. To this end, the LCFF is to be managed by the local districts' Local Control Accountability Plan (LCAP), which gives local districts the ability to set goals, plan actions, and assign their funding and resources toward the best education in their areas. This concept of local control should provide greater flexibility in the expenditure of funds, without being restricted to the categoricals identified by the state (see Chapters Two and Seven for more information on LCAP). To continue to be qualified to receive LCFF funds, schools and districts must exhibit responsible management of funds used in the service of students. To assist in better representing a school's achievements, the state now operates the California Accountability Model and Dashboard, providing charts and graphs to better visually represent school achievements.

Under LCFF, there is a focus on providing additional funding for school districts that have higher student needs, specifically large numbers of English Learners and schools with high numbers and percentages of socioeconomically disadvantaged students. This is an attempt to provide for greater equity and social justice for all students. Under LCFF, school districts all receive a "base grant," based on the total number of students in the school district. A second level of funding, called a "supplemental grant," adds 35% of the base grant calculated on the number of students who are English Learners or economically disadvantaged in the district. Finally, a "concentration grant" of 35% of the base funding goes to districts whose English Language Learners or socioeconomically disadvantaged students are above 50% of the district's enrollment. A key point to note on these calculations is the concept of "unduplicated students," meaning that a district does not receive twice the amount of funding for a student who is both an English Learner and is economically disadvantaged. Each student only counts once for the supplemental and concentration grants. The LCFF, then, provides additional funding for districts to serve students who need the additional support, with districts that have larger percentages of disadvantaged or English Learner students receiving a greater amount of funding. An examination of the funding for two districts in the same general location—Torrance and Downey, both in the Los Angeles basin—will illustrate how economic status affects state funding (*see Table 3.2*).

Table 3.2 - Effects of Socioeconomic Status on School Funding

	% of Students who are Socioeconomically Disadvantaged	Funding for District Prior to LCFF	Funding for District Prior to LCFF
Downey Unified School District	70.3%	$7,757	$11,034
Torrance Unified School District	29.6%	$8,072	$9,116

Note: Adapted from California Budget Project, 2013.

Issues of Equity and Social Justice

The entire history of funding education in California has been fraught with issues of equity and social justice. Some of these issues have been addressed throughout this chapter, as these are at the heart of funding decisions. The reflective and action-based questions that follow here will ask you, the reader, to consider these issues of equity and social justice within the funding of education in California.

Reflective and Action-Based Questions

1. *A highly debated issue in California educational funding is whether school districts with larger percentages of economically disadvantaged and English Learners should receive more—or less—funding than schools with fewer economically disadvantaged students and English Learners. Consider and then write about these two different views. Should schools with higher percentages of economically disadvantaged and English Learners receive higher funding? Why or why not?*
2. *Describe the role that court cases have played in the evolving educational funding arrangements in California.*

References

California Budget Project. (2013, May). *Moving forward: Addressing inequities in school finance through the Governor's Local Control Funding Formula.* Sacramento: Author.

Durbin, J. E. (1972). Equal protection and public school financing: Serrano v Priest. *Loyola of Los Angeles Law Review,* 162–192. Retrieved from https://digitalcommons.lmu.edu/cgi/viewcontent.cgi?referer=https://search.yahoo.com/&httpsredir=1&article=1090&context=llr

Murphy, P., & Paluch, J. (2018, November). *Financing California's public schools.* San Francisco: Public Policy Institute of California. Retrieved from https://www.ppic.org/publication/financing-californias-public-schools/

Oakes, J., & Lipton, M. (2004). Schools that shock the conscience: Williams v California and the struggle for education on equal terms fifty years after Brown. *Berkeley Journal of African-American Law & Policy, 6*(2), 234–258.

U.S. Department of Education. (2011, November 30). *More than 40% of low-income schools don't get a fair share of state and local funds, Department of Education Research finds.* Retrieved from https://www.ed.gov/news/press-releases/more-40-low-income-schools-dont-get-fair-share-state-and-local-funds-department-education-research-finds

CHAPTER FOUR

Curriculum, Content Standards, and Instructional Materials

Guiding Questions

1. *What is the relationship between content standards, curriculum, and instructional materials?*
2. *What is the process for adopting a new curriculum?*
3. *In what ways can textbooks show a bias toward certain groups?*

Introduction

Curriculum, content standards, and instructional materials are designed to both address the changing context of California and to meet state and federal law. Curricular changes are often developed through a collaboration between communities and policy makers. This chapter begins with a brief description of how California selected its curriculum in the late 1800s, then moves to a discussion of the current Common Core movement (for more see Chapter Two), which frames California's content standards, curriculum frameworks, and instructional materials. California's own curriculum trends, which are based on the demographics and social context of the state over time, are also discussed. Included is a description of how textbooks are selected, who has the power to select them, and how to evaluate the instructional materials for bias. Of particular interest in California is the fact that it is called a "textbook adoption state," which lets the state select the instructional materials that will be allowed in the schools, and the school districts select from those approved materials. California wields an important influence in how textbooks and textbook series are created, as California, Texas, and Florida account for almost one-third of the textbook sales in America.

Curriculum History in California

Beginning in 1863, California was one of the first states to institute "The Uniform Plan" to adopt its curriculum materials. The Uniform Plan meant that the State Board of Education approved and adopted a series of textbooks, not local schools or school districts. Schools and school districts across the state had to adopt this series of textbooks, to provide uniformity in the education of the children of the state.

The first set of textbooks adopted was called the Willson's Series of Readers, but shortly afterward the famous McGuffey's Series of Readers became the statewide approved series for California in 1870. This brought California into alignment with popular educational practices in the rest of the country, as 80% of all students in the country either had been or were being educated with McGuffey's Readers (for a description of the McGuffey's Readers, along with sample pages from the original reader, see http://www.alpha-phonics.com/guffy.htm.)

In 1874, the State Board of Education decided to reconsider the appropriateness of the currently adopted textbooks, and decided to examine some new options, this time allowing textbook publishers to compete for their selection. The Board moved away from McGuffey's and instead selected the Pacific Coast Readers. This seems like a reasonable approach, to use a series of textbooks with a Pacific Coast flavor. But a judge in 1875 declared the adoption of Pacific Coast Readers as null and void because they did not give six months' notice of the proposed change. Therefore, a bill was passed in 1875 requiring that the state move back to McGuffey's Readers.

Current Content Standards

The California Department of Education (CDE) lays out the definition of content standards: "Educational content standards describe what students should know and be able to do in each subject at each grade" (https://www.cde.ca.gov/ci/cr/cf/imfrpfaq1.asp). The CDE further describes that "Content standards were designed to encourage the highest achievement of every student, by defining the knowledge, concepts, and skills that students should acquire at each grade level" (https://www.cde.ca.gov/be/st/ss/index.asp). Thus content standards serve as the key organizational factor in determining what will be taught in California's K-12 schools, and what will be the level of achievement expected for each content area (see Chapter Seven for further discussion of assessment and accountability). Content standards are determined by the California State Board of Education (SBE).

Common Core

The Common Core State Standards ("Common Core") in English Language Arts/Literacy and Mathematics were developed in 2010 to better prepare K-12 students for college and careers. Led by the Council of Chief State School Officers and the National Governors Association, the development of Common Core involved educational leaders, administrators, teachers, and the governors of 48 states, making it a wide-ranging and immensely impactful set of standards. The concerns driving the development of the Common Core were that under previous reform efforts (such as No Child Left Behind), student achievement was not improving, and that U.S. students were scoring lower on standardized tests than students from other countries, placing the United States low on the international scale for education (see Chapter Seven for an examination and discussion of whether standardized tests accurately and equitably reflect a student's knowledge). An additional concern was that each state had its own standards, of inconsistent quality and achievement results. With 45 states currently having adopted Common Core, students can be more assured that if they were to move to different districts or even into other states, the standards for academic achievement would be roughly the same.

In addition to English and Mathematics, states utilizing Common Core standards must integrate what is commonly called 21st Century Skills into the curriculum, including such interdisciplinary themes as global awareness; financial, economic, business, and entrepreneurial literacy; civil literacy; health literacy; and environmental literacy. Thus Common Core attempts to help students achieve success in topics of importance in our current social, economic, and political climate.

California responded as one of 45 states to adopt Common Core, and with that came the need to develop curriculum and assessment to both teach and measure the achievement of the new standards. All content standards, curriculum frameworks, and instructional materials must now align with the principles of Common Core. Due to the enormity of the task of revising so much of what is taught in K-12 education, California spent $1.25 billion in its first year to help implement the Common Core-necessitated changes, including new instructional materials, teacher training on the new standards and materials, and improved technology in the form of new devices and accessories to help students learn (Legislative Analyst's Office, 2016). The California Department of Education has developed many online materials to help teachers, parents, students, and community members to better understand the tenets and practices of Common Core (*see Figure 4.1*) and has developed the "California English Learner Roadmap" to provide guidance for school districts' work with English Language Learners (Hakuta, 2018).

FIGURE 4.1 - COMMON CORE RESOURCES

> The California Department of Education has created the *Common Core Channel*, a set of videos and related resources to assist teachers, communities, and parents understand the K-12 California Common Core State Standards, found at https://www.cde.ca.gov/re/cc/commoncorechannel.asp. Additionally, individual school districts throughout the state have created webpages to help explain Common Core, including the standards themselves, explanatory videos, and lesson and unit plans that meet the Common Core Standards (these can be found on the CDE *California Spotlight* website at https://www.cde.ca.gov/re/cc/caspotlight.asp).

Examples of California's Common Core Content Standards

Aligned with research and theory on child and adolescent cognitive development, the standards require a differing level of understanding at each grade level. Each set of content standards provides a thorough discussion of how students learn at different age levels, and how those developmental processes allow students to learn different content at different grade levels. The content standards also include a glossary of terms to help teachers, students, and families/community members understand the content standards. With all of this included in the standards, they are, as can be expected, quite lengthy. For example, the Mathematics content standards are 900 pages in length. Content standards have been developed for 11 content areas: (a) English Language Arts, (b) Mathematics, (c) English Language Development, (d) Career Technical Education, (e) Health Education, (f) History-Social Science, (g) Model School Library, (h) Physical Education, (i) Science, (j) Visual and Performing Arts, and (k) World Language. As of early 2019, content standards are being developed for Computer Science. Next will be an example of content standards from the field of Mathematics.

Example: Mathematics content standards. Mathematical content standards "address both 'habits of mind' that students should develop to foster mathematical understanding and expertise and skills and knowledge—what students need to know and be able to do" (CDE, 2013, January, p. 2). In laying out distinct sets of standards for grade levels K-12, the standards require very specific types of mathematical understandings at different developmental levels.

In Grade 1, students are expected to learn "Operations and Algebraic Thinking," "Number and Operations in Base Ten," "Measurement and Data," and "Geometry." Of course, at Grade 1, students will not be expected to fully understand each of these topics, but rather are introduced to the topics in ways appropriate to their cognitive abilities. As an example, under "Operations and Algebraic Thinking," students are expected to

> Use addition and subtraction within 20 to solve word problems involving situations of adding to, taking from, putting together, taking apart, and comparing, with unknowns in all positions, e.g. by using objects, drawings, and equations with a symbol for the unknown number to represent the problem. (CDE, 2013, January, p. 91)

As can be seen in this single example, the content standards are very specific, and lead to clear paths to assessing student knowledge.

At the other end of the spectrum, Calculus has its own set of standards for the upper grade levels of high school. Similar to the early grade level, it can be seen that the standards expect extremely specific types of knowledge.

> 1.0 Students demonstrate knowledge of both the formal definition and the graphical interpretation of limit of values of functions. This knowledge includes one-sided limits, infinite limits, and limits at infinity. Students know the definition of convergence and divergence of a function as the domain variable approaches either a number or infinity . . . Students prove and use special limits, such as the limits of (sin(x))/x and (1–cos(x))/x as x tends to 0. (CDE, 2013, January, p. 116).

With such attention to detail, the content standards are at the heart of both curriculum and instructional materials, which all are intended help teachers to teach and students to learn these content standards.

Current Curriculum Frameworks

The CDE explains:

> Curriculum frameworks offer guidance for implementing content standards. Frameworks describe the curriculum and instruction necessary to help students achieve proficiency, and they specify the design of instructional materials and professional development. Further, they provide guidelines and selected research-based approaches for implementing instruction to ensure optimal benefits for all students. (https://www.cde.ca.gov/ci/cr/cf/imfrpfaq1.asp)

Most of the content standards have curriculum frameworks to assist educators, including Career Technical Education Framework, English Language Arts Framework, Health Education Framework, History-Social Science Framework, Mathematics Framework, Physical Education Framework, Science Framework, and Visual and Performing Arts Framework. It is these curriculum frameworks that set out the curriculum for each grade level. The frameworks are used by schools to determine which classes should be offered and which curriculum and instructional materials should be used. The curriculum in each content area follows the developmental levels of children and youth, and thus become more complex from kindergarten through to 12th grade. Additionally, the frameworks offer guidance on assessing student learning in that curricular area, suggested instructional practices, and access and equity within the curriculum.

Example: History-Social Science Framework (*see Figure 4.2 for list of topics at each grade level https://www.cde.ca.gov/ci/hs/cf/hssframework.asp—note that this is the most recent framework, from 2016—it is subject to change*).

Within the Curriculum Frameworks are sets of guidance on successful instructional strategies used to teach the subject matter, drawn from research on best practices. In one example, the History-Social Science Framework offers the following guidance for a lesson:

1. *Use a central investigative question to focus the students' attention*
2. *Introduction, have students work together to study documents, provide graphic organizers to assist student learning*
3. *Question review, ensure that all students understand the question*
4. *Specific instructions for students to complete the task*

Figure 4.2 - History-Social Science Curriculum Framework Outline

Kindergarten
- Learning and Working Now and Long Ago

Grade One
- A Child's Place in Time and Space

Grade Two
- People Who Make a Difference

Grade Three
- Continuity and Change

Grade Four
- California: A Changing State

Grade Five
- United States History and Geography: Making a New Nation

Grade Six
- World History and Geography: Ancient Civilizations

Grade Seven
- World History and Geography: Medieval and Early Modern Times

Grade Eight
- United States History and Geography: Growth and Conflict

Grade Nine
- Elective Courses in History-Social Science

Grade Ten
- World History, Culture, and Geography: The Modern World

Grade Eleven
- United States History and Geography: Continuity and Change in Modern United States History

Grade Twelve
- Principles of American Democracy (one semester)
- Principles of Economics (one semester)

With the content standards and curriculum frameworks in place, we can now move to the instructional materials themselves.

Current Instructional Materials

"Instructional materials" means all materials that are designed for use by pupils and their teachers as a learning resource and help pupils to acquire facts, skills, or opinions or to develop cognitive processes. Instructional materials may be printed or non-printed, and may include textbooks, technology-based materials, other educational materials, and tests. (https://www.cde.ca.gov/ci/cr/cf/imfrpfaq1.asp)

California's Instructional Quality Commission (ITQ) is the organization that reviews and recommends curriculum. ITQ is comprised of 18 members and includes current and former teachers, K-12 principals and vice principals, and one state senator and one state House of Representatives member. ITQ receives textbooks and book series from publishers, reviews and evaluates the materials, and makes recommendations to adopt or reject each set of materials. Once the recommendations have been received, the State Board of Education reviews, approves, and recommends instructional materials for school districts. However, school districts may adopt supplemental materials if they meet a list of requirements in their adoption of the materials. One, the materials must align with the state content standards. Two, the process of reviewing the materials locally must include a majority of members who are classroom teachers in the subject area.

California Curriculum Movements

Since curriculum can change from year to year, there is much room for improvement of the curriculum to meet the current needs of the state. The two examples discussed next are representative of how the state chooses and changes its curriculum over time. Note that these changes are directly related to the Political Influences on Education (*see Chapter Two*).

AB-2016 Ethnic Studies Model Curriculum

We can learn about the multifaceted efforts to pass education law by tracing the development of Assembly Bill 2016—Ethnic Studies Curriculum Model. Signed into law in 2016, AB-2016 both requires that an Ethnic Studies curriculum be developed for the state and encourages school districts to adopt and use the new curriculum. The passage of this bill was the result of many years of gatherings of teachers, professors, and community activities (Allender & Berta-Avila, 2016). Evidence was provided to legislators that when students experience a curriculum that values their own histories, cultures, and traditions, they achieve both academic and personal gains. Comprehensive evidence demonstrates that K-12 students taking an Ethnic Studies course show both academic and personal growth, including increased GPA, fewer absences, and a higher graduation rate (Cabrera, Milem, Jaquette, & Marx, 2014; Dee & Penner, 2017; Sleeter, 2011).

Moving to the formal political structure and process for developing and passing a law, the following table shows the complex process of formalizing the new curriculum. Once the bill was passed and signed by the governor, a year-long set of official state department meetings and planning sessions were convened to actually develop the new Model Ethnic Studies Curriculum. This is an example of (a) how teachers can contribute to the passage of education law for the improvement of their fields, and (b) the political structure and process that is commonly followed for the final passage of a bill, as well as the follow-ups required to turn the law into practice. In reality, an early version of this effort was proposed in 2002, so there was much effort on the part of educators, students, community members, and legislators between 2002 and the passage of AB 2016. *Table 4.1 on page 52 describes the most recent steps, beginning in 2014.*

This list of actions taken to pass and implement the AB-2016 Ethnic Studies Model Curriculum is not meant to intimidate educators (although it is quite a lengthy process), but rather to let educators and community members understand that they can play an important role in the development of state law and of K-12 curriculum.

TABLE 4.1 -
STEPS IN DEVELOPING ETHNIC STUDIES CURRICULUM

Date	Steps in Process
2014–2016	Ethnic Studies taught in several districts throughout California, including Oxnard, Coachella Valley, and San Francisco, among others.
2014	Ethnic Studies Now Coalition formed to advocate for increasing Ethnic Studies curriculum in California schools and colleges.
2014–present	Meetings of teachers, professors, and community members. Petitions gathered online to submit to legislators and governor. Members of Ethnic Studies Now Coalition testify at the state capitol on the importance of Ethnic Studies.
2016, February	AB-2016 proposed by Assembly member Luis A. Alejo, Salinas.
2016, June	AB-2016 approved by House of Representatives.
2016, August	AB-2016 approved by Senate.
2016, September	AB-2016 is signed by Governor Jerry Brown. Section 51226.7 added to Education Code.
2016–2017 school year	Ethnic Studies Now reports that 17,354 students were enrolled in Ethnic Studies courses statewide.
2018, January	CDE holds a "public input webinar" to gather the public's ideas about the newly developing curriculum.
2018, May	Instructional Quality Committee (IQC) recommends time line and Model Curriculum Advisory Committee (MCAC) application guidelines.
2018, July	State Board of Education approves IQC's recommendations.
2018, August–October	Recruitment of MCAC members.
2018, November	IQC recommends MCAC members.
2019, January	State Board of Education appoints MCAC members.
2019, February, March, April	MCAC holds three meetings to develop draft curriculum.
2019, May	IQC reviews draft curriculum and approves for public review.
2019, June–August	IQC posts draft curriculum on CDE website for public feedback.
2019, September	IQC analyzes public feedback and revises draft curriculum.
2019, November	IQC recommends draft curriculum to State Board of Education.
2020, by March	State Board of Education reviews curriculum.
2020, March 31	Final Ethnic Studies Model Curriculum approved.

SB 48 (2011)—The FAIR Education Act

The passage of the FAIR Education Act was a similarly lengthy process that involved educators and community members (full time line can be seen at http://www.faireducationact.com/about-fair/a-fair-ed-history/). The FAIR Act requires California curriculum to provide Fair, Accurate, Inclusive and Respectful (FAIR) inclusion of contributions of various groups in the history of California and the United States. While the California Education Code already required the study of many racial and ethnic groups within the social studies curriculum, the FAIR Act provides further inclusivity by newly mandating that the curriculum provide respectful information about members of the LGBT community and people with disabilities. This makes California the first state to include this provision in state law. In Education Code 51204.5, the state curriculum now must include

> a study of the role and contributions of both men and women, Native Americans, African Americans, Mexican Americans, Asian Americans, Pacific Islanders, European Americans, lesbian, gay, bisexual, and transgender Americans, persons with disabilities, and members of other ethnic and cultural groups, to the economic, political, and social development of California and the United States of America, with particular emphasis on portraying the role of these groups in contemporary society.

Many organizations and coalitions worked to advocate for this FAIR inclusion of all within California curriculum, including Our Family Coalition, Equality California, the ACLU, the Youth-led GSA Network, and Youth Organizing–Disabled & Proud, among others. Similar to the Ethnic Studies effort, organizations and individuals advocated for the passage of the law, including letters and testimonies presented to the legislature. The time line for developing new curriculum is similar, also, to the Ethnic Studies efforts (*see Figure 4.3*).

These are merely two examples of the process followed, both informal advocacy and formal political structure, to change the curriculum in California. This process allows for public input and for those invested in the issues to make a difference at the statewide level.

Figure 4.3 - Steps in Developing the FAIR Act Curriculum

- 2010—Senator Mark Leno introduced SB 48, the FAIR Education Act
- 2011—passed through the legislature and signed by the governor
- 2012–2014—draft of revised History Social Science Framework prepared
- 2014—over 700 public comments about the draft Framework received by CDE during public review
- 2016—State Board of Education adopts revised History Social Science Framework
- 2017—Instructional Quality Commission approves and recommends LGBT and disabilities-inclusive framework

Issues of Equity and Social Justice

Of critical importance in any discussion of curriculum, standards, and instructional materials is the question of "who?" Who creates the curriculum? Who selects the textbooks? Who decides what students will learn, through the choice of curriculum and instructional materials? And most importantly, who is left out of these decisions?

Native American Curriculum and Instructional Materials

Reynolds (2014) examined California's 4th grade social studies textbooks from throughout the twentieth century, to see if there were any changes in how the textbooks represented the California missions and Native Americans over time. The answer was: yes.

- 1922. "The friars treated the Indians kindly, as if they were children. But sometimes the Indians ran away, because they did not like to work, and preferred the free life of the mountains and valleys."
- 1948. "Everyone was happy and busy. Padre Serra went from garden to field. He preached... In 14 years, he had helped change a large part of the desert into rich farm land. He had helped make thousands of poor, half-starved savages into happy, bustling workers."
- 1965. "The Indians at the missions ate more regularly than when they were wild. The padres took care of them in many ways. The Indians had the feeling of being part of something much bigger than the old Indian village. They learned to do many things as the Spaniards did. They learned many new skills. On the whole, they must have felt better off than before."
- 1991. "Mission Indians were not allowed to return to their tribes once they agreed to take part in mission life... Many Indians died of diseases brought by the Spanish. When crops failed, Indians didn't have enough to eat. Some became sick from the change in their diet on the missions. By the end of the mission period, the California Indian population was half the size that it had been when Father Serra raised his first cross at San Diego Mission."

As can be seen, the curriculum taught California students for over a century that Native Americans were wild, savages, and quite content to be forced into labor and removed from their homes. As Eargle (2016) explains, "textbooks include the perpetuation of myths, the marginalization of under-represented groups, an aversion to controversy" (p. 297). Critical Race Theory (CRT) has been utilized to help underrepresented groups have their voices heard in decisions about how they are represented in the curriculum and in textbooks. CRT recognizes that racism has influenced institutions and lives within the United States and that it has framed policy and practice. As Yosso (2005) describes, CRT "focuses on and learns from the array of cultural knowledge, skills, abilities and contacts possessed by socially marginalized groups that often go unrecognized and unacknowledged" (p. 69). We can see CRT being utilized by the groups that advocated for the Ethnic Studies and LGBTQ+ curriculum, described earlier.

Similarly, Native American communities and educators have worked together to advocate for the passage of AB-738, in 2017 (which also added Section 51226.9–Native American Curriculum to the Education Code). Most importantly, AB-738 requires that the State Board of Education work collaboratively with Native American groups and educators in developing new curriculum and content standards.

> (a)(1) The Instructional Quality Commission shall develop, and the state board shall adopt, modify, or revise, a model curriculum in Native American studies to ensure quality courses of study in Native American studies. The model curriculum shall be developed with participation from federally recognized Native American tribes located in California, California Native American tribes, faculty of Native American studies programs at universities and colleges with Native American studies programs, and a group of representatives of local educational agencies, a majority of whom are kindergarten to grade 12, inclusive, teachers who have relevant experiences or education backgrounds in the study and teaching of Native American studies. The Governor's Tribal Advisor, the Native American Heritage Commission, and the department shall assist the Instructional Quality Commission

> in statewide tribal consultations with federally recognized Native American tribes located in California and California Native American tribes.

This effort was catalyzed by a number of groups, including the California Indian History Curriculum Coalition of educators, native activists, and tribal scholars. "The goal of the Coalition is to promote the creation, adoption and implementation of California Indian-vetted curricula . . . to infuse California Indian voice in the content of what our children learn in school" (https://www.csus.edu/coe/cic/).

Williams Case

In addition to the questions listed previously regarding who makes the curricular decisions and who writes the stories of groups, a critical question for California is: Who has access to textbooks? To qualified teachers? To clean and adequate facilities? These questions were at the heart of one of the most significant recent cases, *Williams v California,* filed in 1997 and with improvements signed by the governor in 2004 (see more about the Williams case in Chapters Two and Three). The case brought attention to the severe inequities in availability of textbooks, qualified teachers, and clean and adequate facilities, based on race and socioeconomic status. The findings regarding instructional materials were that "teachers working in schools with the highest concentrations of poor children were also most likely to have inadequate materials" (Oakes & Lipton, 2004, p. 241). (*See Table 4.2 for the data.*)

TABLE 4.2 - WILLIAMS ACT FINDINGS

	Schools with the highest poverty (n = 216)	Schools with the lowest poverty (n = 217)
Not enough textbooks to use in the classroom	12%	11%
Not enough textbooks for students to take home	42%	27%
Textbooks are of fair or poor quality	20%	9%
Textbooks have fair or poor coverage of state standards	21%	15%

(*Note:* Table adapted from Oakes & Lipton, 2004, p. 241)

While it is concerning that in 2004 only one out of four schools in low poverty areas had enough textbooks for students to take home, it is alarming that nearly half of students attending schools in high poverty areas could not take home textbooks. In other words, "Textbook shortages are the greatest in low-income schools" (Oakes & Lipton, 2004, p. 241). As a result of the Williams case and settlement, every public school in California now is reviewed yearly for adherence to providing both enough and quality textbooks, and the results of these reviews are posted publicly in the School Accountability Report Cards.

Evaluating Curriculum for Bias

The California Department of Education (2013) has created a set of guidelines to help educators evaluate instructional materials for potential inaccuracies and biases that might cause harm to groups. All curricula approved by the CDE for use in California have been evaluated and meet these guidelines for appropriate representation of topics and groups. It is important to note that when there are changes in curriculum, all new materials must meet these guidelines. California law (Education Code) requires that

> instructional materials portray accurately and equitably the cultural and racial diversity of American society; the male and female roles; and the contributions of minority groups, the disabled, gay, lesbian, bisexual, and transgendered individuals, and males and females to the development of California and the United States. These requirements imply that instructional materials must also help students to understand both the historical roles and the contributions of women and minorities in other societies; the forces that shaped those roles and contributions; and how and why the roles and contributions of contemporary American women and minorities differ from those of women and minorities at other times and in other cultures. (CDE, 2013, September 5, p. 2)

The guidelines identify 13 topics and groups that are most commonly misrepresented in instructional materials, where bias occurs most frequently. The purpose and method for examining the representation of each topic and group are presented next, directly from the California Department of Education guidelines.

1. Male and Female Roles
Education Code Sections 51501, 60040(a), and 60044(a)
Purpose. The standards promote the individual development and self-esteem of each student, regardless of gender.
Method. The standards will be achieved by portraying people of both sexes in the full range of their human potential in all societal roles. (p. 4)

2. Ethnic and Cultural Groups
Education Code Sections 51501, 60040(b), and 60044(a)
Purpose. The standards project the cultural diversity of society; instill in each child a sense of pride in his or her heritage; develop a feeling of self-worth related to equality of opportunity; eradicate the roots of prejudice; and thereby encourage the optimal individual development of each student.
Method. The standards will be achieved by including a fair representation of majority and minority group characters portrayed in a wide variety of occupations and roles, including cultural and artistic roles. (pp. 5–6)

3. Sexual Orientation and Gender Identity
Education Code Sections 50501, 60040(b), and 60044(a)
Purpose. The standards promote the individual development and self-esteem of each student, regardless of sexual orientation or gender identity.
Method. The standards will be achieved by avoiding pejorative descriptions of people based upon their sexual orientation or gender identity, and by including references to the contributions of persons of diverse sexual orientations and gender identities. (p. 7)

4. Older Persons and the Aging Process

Approved by the State Board of Education on July 12, 1979

Purpose. The standards promote the development of a healthy perception of older people and a concept of the aging process as a natural phenomenon.

Method. The standards will be achieved by depicting older persons and their activities and contributions as a vital part of society. (p. 8)

5. People with Disabilities

Education Code Sections 50501, 60040(b), and 60044(a)

Purpose. The standards promote the development of a perception of people with disabilities that is clear and undistorted, without fear, distrust, loathing, amusement, ridicule, contempt, or pity.

Method. The standards will be achieved by depicting the involvement, activities, and contributions of people with disabilities as an integral part of society. (pp. 8–9)

6. Entrepreneur and Labor

Education Code Sections 60040(c) and 60044(a)

Purpose. The standards develop in students an unbiased view of the functions of the entrepreneur and of labor in American society.

Method. The standards will be achieved by presenting, when it is appropriate to do so, a balanced picture of the roles of entrepreneurs, managers, and labor (as represented by workers and their organizations) in the American free enterprise system. (p. 9)

7. Religion

Education Code Sections 51501, 60044(a) and (b)

Purpose. The standards enable all students to become aware and accepting of religious diversity while being allowed to remain secure in any religious beliefs they may already have.

Method. The standards will be achieved by depicting, when appropriate, the diversity of religious beliefs held in the United States and California, as well as in other societies, without displaying bias toward or prejudice against any of those beliefs or religious beliefs in general. (p. 10)

8. Ecology and the Environment

Education Code Section 60041(a)

Purpose. The standards develop in all students a sense of responsibility for the protection and improvement of the natural environment as much as possible.

Method. The standards will be achieved by emphasizing to students, when appropriate, issues related to ecology and the environment and what ordinary citizens can do to contribute to the resolution of those issues. (pp. 10–11)

9. Dangerous Substances

Education Code Section 60041(b)

Purpose. The standards provide all students knowledge of the various uses and misuses of dangerous substances.

Method. The standards will be achieved by presenting factual information regarding the effects of dangerous substances. (p. 11)

10. Thrift, Fire Prevention, and Humane Treatment of Animals and People

Education Code Section 60042

Purpose. The standards instill in all students some basic values: thrift, fire prevention, and humane treatment of animals and people.

Method. The standards will be achieved by demonstrating the connection between these values and both everyday and extraordinary occurrences in human living and history. (pp. 11–12)

11. Declaration of Independence and Constitution of the United States

Education Code Section 60043

These standards need to be met only when students are at a level appropriate to the comprehension of the Declaration of Independence

and the U.S. Constitution. In addition, the standards apply only to instructional materials for social science, history, or civics classes.
The Declaration of Independence should be presented.
The United States Constitution should be included. (p. 12)

12. Brand Names and Corporate Logos
Education Code Sections 60048 and 60200
Guidelines approved by the State Board of Education on January 13, 2000
Purpose. The standards prevent unfair exposure of any privately produced product and students' exposure to unnecessary advertising.
Method. The standards will be achieved by omitting, whenever possible, illustrations of or references to private producers or their products.
Guidelines for Exemptions. Exemptions to the standards regarding brand names and corporate logos are allowable . . . (p. 13)

13. Nutrition and Physical Activity
Approved by the State Board of Education on January 10, 1986 and updated on May 8, 2013
Purpose. The standards accustom students to seeing and dealing with representations of nutritious foods and foster a positive attitude toward physical activity; healthy eating and physical activity are essential to children's health and well-being.
Method. The standards will be achieved by emphasizing foods of high nutritional value and regular physical activity when it is appropriate to do so. (p. 15)

These guidelines are helpful in understanding what would be considered inaccurate or biased materials. In particular, those who want to evaluate materials are encouraged to examine how the following are portrayed in materials. In each of these cases, exceptions can be made for special circumstances such as studying social history, when the class examines historical materials that inaccurately portrayed women and people of color.

1. *Adverse reflection.* Instructional materials must not include written descriptions, illustrations, captions or labels, or rejoinders that would stereotype, demean, or patronize any groups, such as related to gender, ethnicity, etc.

2. *Equal portrayal.* Instructional materials that include written descriptions or illustrations must refer to or illustrate members of the various groups (i.e., gender, disabilities, etc.) "approximately evenly, in both number and degree of importance, except as limited by accuracy or special purpose" (p. 5). Additionally, the roles and contributions of the various groups (i.e., based on sexual orientation or gender identity) must portray a "fair proportion" (p. 7) of the contributions of the various groups.

3. *Occupations.* Instructional materials that cover a wide variety of occupations or roles (i.e., executives, parents, nurses, firefighters, etc.) must present the various groups taking part in the full range of these roles.

4. *Achievements.* In instructional materials that present history, current events, or achievements in the wide range of fields within society, the contributions of the various groups should be represented in the materials "when it is historically accurate to do so" (p. 6).

5. *Mental and physical activities.* Members from each of the groups "should be depicted in roles in which they are being mentally and physically active, being creative, solving problems, and experiencing success and failure in those roles" (p. 5).

6. *Traditional and nontraditional activities, customs, and lifestyles.* When activities, customs, traditions, and lifestyles are represented in text and illustrations, members of the various groups should be portrayed in ways that do not represent those as being undesirable or unusual. A balance should be portrayed between nontraditional or ancestral activities and traditional activities for

each group, so that no group is portrayed only as being either traditional and appropriate or cultural or nontraditional, meaning inappropriate.

7. *Socioeconomic settings.* People from the various groups should be included in text and illustrations as being within the same range of socioeconomic settings.

Reflective and Action-Based Questions

1. *Examine a K-12 textbook, in any subject matter, and analyze it using the guidelines provided for evaluating a textbook for bias. For each category #1–13, describe your findings related to potential bias.*
2. *Using the CDE website, select a Curriculum Framework for one subject matter and one grade. Create a lesson or unit plan that will present the information within that Curriculum Framework.*
3. *Selecting your own educational topic of interest, identify any local or state organizations that serve to advocate for that topic.*

References

Allender, D., & Berta-Avila, M. (2016). *A Capitol City case study of curriculum transformation and community empowerment: Ethnic Studies Now-Sacramento.* Center XChange https://ucla.app.box.com/v/Ethnic-Studies-Now-Sacramento

Cabrera, N. L., Milem, J. F., Jaquette, O., & Marx, R. W. (2014). Missing the (student achievement) forest for all the (political) trees: Empiricism and the Mexican American studies controversy in Tucson. *American Educational Research Journal, 51*(6), 1084–1118.

California Department of Education. (2013, January). *California Common Core State Standards: Mathematics.* Retrieved from https://www.cde.ca.gov/be/st/ss/documents/ccssmathstandardaug2013.pdf

California Department of Education. (2013, September 5). *Standards for evaluating instructional materials for social content.* Retrieved from https://www.cde.ca.gov/ci/cr/cf/documents/socialcontent2013.doc

Dee, T. S., & Penner, E. K. (2017). The causal effects of cultural relevance: Evidence from an ethnic studies curriculum. *American Educational Research Journal, 54*(1), 127–166.

Eargle, J. C. (2016). The dominant narrative of slavery in South Carolina's history standards. *The Journal of Social Studies Research, 40*, 295–307.

Hakuta, K. (2018). *California English Learner roadmap: Strengthening comprehensive educational policies, programs, and practices for English Learners*. Sacramento: California Department of Education.

Legislative Analyst's Office. (2016, June 10). *How did California schools spend Common Core implementation funding?* Retrieved from https://lao.ca.gov/Publications/Report/3483

Oakes, J., & Lipton, M. (2004). Schools that shock the conscience: Williams v California and the struggle for education on equal terms fifty years after Brown. *Berkeley Journal of African-American Law & Policy, 6*(2), 234–258.

Reynolds, C. (2014, September 5). California missions: How textbooks evolved to reflect the plight of Native Americans. *Los Angeles Times*. Retrieved from https://www.latimes.com/travel/california/missions/la-tr-d-missions-textbookwords-20140907-story.html

Sleeter, C. E. (2011). *The academic and social value of ethnic studies: A research review.* Washington, DC: National Education Association.

Yosso, T. J. (2005). Whose culture has capital? A critical race theory discussion of community cultural wealth. *Race, Ethnicity and Education, 8*(1), 69–91.

CHAPTER FIVE

Assessment and Accountability: Practices and Issues

Guiding Questions

1. *What are two types of assessment?*
2. *What is high-stakes testing, and what are the consequences of utilizing a high-stakes testing system?*
3. *Why is testing called a "big business?"*

Introduction

ASSESSMENT HAS HISTORICALLY referred to determining how much a student has learned within a classroom. But since the latter half of the 1960s, assessment has grown into a full-blown system of accountability that uses testing to judge students, teachers, principals, school districts, states, and even nations against a set of norms and against each other (see Chapter Two for further discussion on this topic). This chapter describes the concept of accountability, the corresponding focus on assessment, and some of the problems with enacting a system of "high-stakes testing."

Accountability

Since the Elementary and Secondary Education Act was signed in 1965, the United States has moved toward a test-based concept of accountability. As described in Chapter Two, from the 1960s through the early 2000s, state after state adopted more stringent test-based definitions of accountability, with California leading the way in many cases. The primary reasons identified for developing state-wide assessment systems are twofold: equity and accountability. Within this system, test scores are believed to be a good indicator of whether all students are learning equitably, with the goal of reducing or eliminating the "achievement gap" between children of privilege, often White, and students of color, often socioeconomically disadvantaged. But this is only one reason for testing. The other is to hold schools "accountable" to students, parents, communities, and the nation, which is to be measured by student test scores. Since it is important for communities, states, and the nation for schools to educate children well and equitably, over time the measure of accountability has been narrowed into a test score: a single number that will indicate how well a student has learned, and how well a school has fulfilled its obligation of education for its students.

With the system of testing growing in significance, a corresponding system grew along with it: the need to specify what specific information students need to learn, and what level of knowledge should count as having achieved that knowledge. There needed to be both a standardized set of curricula that all would learn (see Chapter Four for further discussion), and an achievement level for which all would strive. Thus, the accountability and testing movement necessarily required standards to which teachers and students would work to achieve. How much should a student know about a topic at each grade level? What would count as having achieved the learning of that material? The California Department of Education website provides a chronological overview of the state's movement toward creating and embedding standards that all students are expected to achieve (see https://www.cde.ca.gov/nr/re/hd/yr96-10tl.asp).

California requires that each school report on a host of school-related information on a School Accountability Report Card (SARC). Each SARC is submitted to the school district and then posted online for public access. The goal of instituting the SARC requirements is to help parents and community members better understand their neighborhood school, to hold the schools accountable to their students' families and communities, and to fulfill a number of required data reporting laws in California (*see Table 5.1 on page 67 for the categories of information required on the SARC*).

TABLE 5.1 - SCHOOL ACCOUNTABILITY REPORT CARDS

Category of Information	Uses of Information for Accountability
School description	For parents to better understand school culture
Student enrollment	For Local Control Funding Formula
Conditions of Learning: • Teacher credentials and grade level/subject matter assignments	Originally created as a result of NCLB Fulfills the Williams Case requirement of noting teacher qualifications
Conditions of Learning: • Quality, currency, and availability of textbooks and instructional materials	Fulfills the Williams Case requirement of noting the status and availability of a school's textbooks
Conditions of Learning: • School facility conditions and planned improvements	Fulfills the Williams Case requirement of noting school infrastructure issues
Pupil Outcomes • CAASSP—percent of students meeting or exceeding state standards (overall, Physical Fitness Test, by subject area) • Disaggregated by demographic group	For many uses—all stakeholders who need to see schools being accountable
Engagement • Opportunities for parent involvement	Fulfills the requirement of the Local Control Accountability Plan, which requires parent engagement in school planning and other leadership committees
Engagement • School safety plan	For school personnel to ensure safety
Suspensions and expulsions	For Local Control Funding Formula
"Other" • Counselors and other support staff areas, class size	For reports to district and CDE
Professional development provided for teachers	For teachers to remain current
Budget • Teacher and administrator salaries • Per pupil funding	California law requires that all government employee salaries be made publicly accessible
Types of services provided • Additional services outside regular classroom instruction	For parents to better understand school culture

Assessment

As described throughout this book, testing has become the primary method of determining a student's level of learning. While assessment was long the purview of the classroom teacher, since the mid-1960s testing has become a way to judge the achievement of a school as well. Before describing the testing conducted in California, it will be helpful to understand two types of tests: criterion-referenced and norm-referenced. *Table 5.2 on page 68 points out the similarities and differences between these types of tests.*

TABLE 5.2 - CRITERION AND NORM-REFERENCED TESTS

	Criterion-Referenced Tests	Norm-Referenced Tests
Purpose	To determine whether a student has achieved the knowledge or skills being taught To determine whether an individual student has learned specific knowledge or skills	To determine how close a student comes to a "normal" range of scores To rank students compared to others taking the same test
Summative or Formative	Can be summative—provides a summary of student learning after a lesson or portion of a school year Can be formative—provides teachers information during a lesson or during the school year	Only summative—provides a summary of student learning after a lesson or portion of a school year
Expected Results	The hope is that all students will "pass" the test, or will score at the "proficient" or higher level on a particular question	There will be a range of student scores (often called a "bell curve"), with some scoring lower and some scoring higher than average
Who Creates Tests	Can be created by publishers or educational agencies Can be created by a teacher	Created by publishers or educational agencies
How Used	Used at the school-wide level to report school's overall achievement level Used to help teacher adjust lessons so that students better understand the material	Used at the school-wide level to report school's overall achievement level Used by individual students to relay their test scores, such as to college admissions offices

High-Stakes Testing in the Time of NCLB

California, and the nation, reached the peak of testing requirements following the passage of the No Child Left Behind Act of 2001, which required schools to be judged based on student test scores. While testing can be very useful to learn about how much a student knows, and that is how testing has served for generations, the time of NCLB (late 1990s through the 2000s) resulted in test scores determining whether teachers and principals kept their jobs, whether outside consultants came in to try to institute new procedures, or even whether a school would close down. This time frame of the late 1990s through the 2000s became known as the time of "high-stakes testing."

Due to the heavy focus on test scores and potential punishments related to high-stakes testing, a number of test preparation activities have ensued. Teachers from the time of NCLB tell stories of the inordinate amount of time spent on preparing their students for the standardized tests so that the students will score well and the school "won't be shut down." Examples include school-wide assemblies or "pep rallies" leading up to the tests; skipping the main curriculum in the time period prior to the tests to teach students "how to take tests"; and setting up an informal system to randomly ask potential test questions to children at recess. Johnson and Johnson (2006) relay the statements of teachers and students from the NCLB time period. Before the school-wide standardized tests, a 4th grade student wrote a note to the teacher: "Dear Mr. Johnson, Happy Birthday. I hope you have fun on your special day... I will try really hard to pass the Leaptest [sic] just for you" (p. 126). Upon completion of the testing period, a different teacher proclaimed "We did it! We survived *the tests*. Even with all the tears and upset stomachs, we survived. Now maybe we can get back to teaching kids" (p. 140).

A national study of 66 of the largest school districts in the nation found that over 400 separate standardized tests have been developed and used in K-12 schools (Hart et al., 2015). At the individual student level, students on average were required to take 112 standardized tests between kindergarten and 12th grade. Remember, standardized tests are norm-referenced, and are created for the purpose of comparing students to a standard or norm, with the same norm expected for all students. This does not include tests that teachers create and give in their classrooms, such as the weekly vocabulary tests common in elementary schools.

How beneficial are these tests to the individual teacher and student? The most benefit would be if teachers could use test scores to better understand how their students are learning, and then to be able to adjust their teaching and materials to better help students learn. One problem with standardized tests is that the results are not immediately known by the teacher. As Hart et al. (2015) note,

> Some 39 percent of districts reported having to wait between two and four months before final state test results were available at the school level, thereby minimizing their utility for instructional purposes. In addition, most state tests are administered in the spring and results come back to the districts after the conclusion of the school year. (p. 11)

California's Standardized Testing Movement, 1997–2010

Testing is big business. The increasing focus on testing over the past 50 years has created a "business relationship between school systems and testing companies . . . State officials thus became and remain contract managers, overseeing a private company assigned the responsibility of creating, printing, and scoring tests" (Dorn, 2007, p. xvii). In 2015, California signed a $240 million, three-year contract with Educational Testing Service (ETS) to administer the state's K-12 standardized tests.

As a leader in the movement to increase testing as a formal way to provide accountability, California established a strict and unyielding state-wide testing system to assess student learning but also to judge schools. Some of the components of the testing system are no longer utilized, while the framework of testing set at the time resulted in some testing practices continuing today. A host of acronyms can explain the testing system of the time, none of which still exist in their original form. The main difference between the "high-stakes testing" framework and the current accountability system developed as a result of ESSA is that current assessment and accountability draws on multiple measures of achievement, not single test scores.

- PSAA—Public Schools Accountability Act of 1999. Provided the framework for all testing functions in K-12 education. (No longer exists)

- STAR—Standardized Testing and Reporting. The set of tests given to all students, with a system for reporting the results publicly. (Replaced by the CAASSP —see below for further description)

- CST—California Standards Tests. Measured student learning of the standards required by the state. (No longer exists in original form)

- API—Academic Performance Index. This was the combining of all students' test scores in a single school into a single number, ranging from 200–1,000. Schools were all supposed to aim for a score of 800. (No longer exists)

- AYP—Academic Year Progress. A measurement of annual school achievement of test score goals. If a school did not reach 800, a target was imposed upon them to achieve 5% growth each year. (No longer exists)
- PI—Program Improvement. For schools that received Title I funding (lowest income schools), if they did not meet the AYP in subsequent years, they would enter into an increasingly severe set of punishments. Consequences began with relatively unobtrusive measures such as revising curriculum, to eventually firing principals and teachers, and finally to the closure of the school or taking it over by an outside agency. This sequence occurred from years 1–5 of not meeting the target AYP. (No longer exists)
- School choice based on test scores. Schools were required to notify parents, in writing, that they can move their children from a Program Improvement school to a school that did meet the test score standards. (No longer exists after ESSA changes)

California's system of testing, and reporting test results, has become the epitome of the notion of high-stakes testing. However, with the signing of the Every School Succeeds Act in 2015, states are allowed to have a bit more leeway in designing tests that get at a deeper understanding of material.

Current Standardized Tests in California

As of 2018, California utilizes a set of assessments for testing student knowledge and skills that fall under the umbrella of California Assessment of Student Performance and Progress (CAASPP) Assessment. The subject areas that make up this overall system are English Language Arts/Literacy, Mathematics, Science, Spanish, and Reading/Language Arts Assessment, along with a few others. Importantly, California provides the option of alternate assessments for students with disabilities. Several of these assessments will be described here.

Smarter Balanced Assessment System

Adopted in conjunction with the Common Core State Standards and Curriculum (see Chapter Four for further discussion of Common Core), Smarter Balanced Assessment goes beyond the traditional paper and pencil tests to incorporate both computer-based tests and performative tests, which allow students to demonstrate their knowledge and skills in ways other than traditional testing. As a system, Smarter Balanced Assessment provides a set of tests that can be used as interim (formative) assessments, summative assessments, and includes a Digital Library that provides a test bank for districts to use. As an integral part of the Common Core, Smarter Balanced Assessment is intended to help measure if students are moving toward college and career readiness.

English Language Proficiency Assessments for California (ELPAC)

As of July 2018, the ELPAC is the required test for California students whose primary language is not English (replacing the previously required California English Language Development Test–CELDT). The ELPAC is given to students whose primary language is not English, within 30 days of first enrolling in school. This provides schools with an assessment of the English language level of new students and helps to determine the best course of instruction. Then, the ELPAC is readministrated annually, until it is determined that the student is reclassified as fluent English proficient, or RFEP. The ELPAC tests students in the areas of listening, speaking, reading, and writing. Because the level of English proficiency plays such a significant role in the student's schooling, including being assigned to various EL instructional models including sometimes outside the regular classroom, there is an effort to help parents understand both the test and how to help their children prepare for the test. The CDE website offers numerous resources for parents, most in English but some in Spanish, including videos, practice tests, and explanations of what ELPAC scores mean.

Physical Fitness Test

Designed by an external company (The Cooper Institute), the FITNESSGRAM is California's selected Physical Fitness Test (PFT) that has been given since the Education Code first required a test in 1996. The PFT measures physical fitness in grades 5, 7, and 9. The PFT results are provided to students to help them understand their level of physical fitness, to parents to help them monitor their child's physical health, and to teachers to help them plan physical fitness activities. Like the other tests, PFT scores are listed on the School Accountability Report Card, for anyone to access online.

Issues of Equity and Social Justice

The impacts of high-stakes testing are felt to differing degrees of severity in schools with privileged families and schools with primarily socioeconomically disadvantaged students and families. Why is this the case? Unfortunately, the differential school experiences of Black and Latino students are currently at their highest in California. In a concept called "resegregation," even when there is no legal segregation based on race or ethnicity, schools are currently moving toward being attended by a high proportion of White and Asian students, or a high proportion of Black and Latino students. Students in these resegregated schools in California rarely interact with one another outside their local community. In other words, Whites and Asians see Whites and Asians daily, and Blacks and Latinos see Blacks and Latinos daily. Currently, California Latino students attend schools that are 84% Black and Latino and that are 75% socioeconomically disadvantaged (Orfield & Ee, 2014). Unfortunately, those percentages are on the rise.

Why does this matter? The Williams Case (discussed previously in Chapters Two and Three) provides a clear set of evidence for the impact of socioeconomic status, which concurrently involves race, on the educational experiences of students in California. As described in Chapter Three, schools with the highest concentration of socioeconomically disadvantaged students of color, specifically Black and Latino, have (a) the highest number of inadequate textbooks and materials, (b) the highest number of teachers not fully certified, and (c) the most critical infrastructure breakdowns and overcrowding (Oakes & Lipton, 2004). To explain further, numerous studies, as well as common sense, have shown that when students attend schools that are under-resourced and under immense pressure to raise test scores, the curriculum gets narrowed to focus on the tests. Orfield and Ee (2014) continue:

> Schools serving low income and segregated neighborhoods have been shown to provide less challenging curricula than schools in more affluent communities, which largely serve white and Asian students. High-stakes testing has hurt minority-segregated schools, as it leads to a focus on learning rote skills and test-taking strategies and often takes the place of creative, engaging teaching. By contrast, students in middle class schools normally have little trouble with high-stakes exams, so these schools and their teachers are able to broaden the curriculum. Segregated schools are also significantly less likely than more affluent schools to offer AP or honors level courses. (p. 21)

How does this tie to test scores? A school full of opportunities for students provides a set of knowledge and experiences that will prepare them to achieve on tests, but more importantly, to move on to college. Fahle and Reardon (2018) explain:

> Why might test scores vary among school districts? . . . students' average test scores are a function of their accumulated educational opportunities in and out of school to learn the tested material. To the extent that these opportunities vary systematically among school districts, district-average test scores will reflect this variation. (p. 222)

In summary, then, "Black and Latino students are strongly concentrated in schools that have far lower quality . . . Conversely, a far larger share of Whites and Asians attend the most highly rated schools and thus are the most prepared for college" (p. 3).

Reflective and Action-Based Questions

1. Select three of the following groups and describe the ways these three groups may use test scores.

Students
Teachers
Parents
Principals
States
Politicians or legislators

2. Trace and discuss the connections between accountability and high-stakes testing.

3. Find your school's School Accountability Report Card (posted online, usually on the school or school district website). In looking at student test results, listed by each demographic group, discuss the differences in test scores among groups. Then, look further at your school to find if there are support services or programs for those students who have experienced the largest gap between the lowest and highest test scores.

References

Dorn, S. (2007). *Accountability Frankenstein: Understanding and taming the monster.* Charlotte, NC: Information Age Publishing.

Fahle, E. M., & Reardon, S. F. (2018). How much do test scores vary among school districts? New estimates using population data, 2009–2015. *Educational Researcher, 47*(4), 221–234.

Hart, R., Casserly, M., Uzzell, R., Palacios, M., Corcoran, A., & Spurgeon, L. (2015, October). *Student testing in America's great city schools: An inventory and preliminary analysis.* Washington, DC: Council of the Great City Schools.

Johnson, D. D., & Johnson, B. (2006). *High stakes: Poverty, testing, and failure in American schools* (2nd ed.). New York: Rowman & Littlefield Publishers, Inc.

Oakes, J., & Lipton, M. (2004). Schools that shock the conscience: Williams v California and the struggle for education on equal terms fifty years after Brown. *Berkeley Journal of African-American Law & Policy, 6*(2), 234–258.

Orfield, G., & Ee, J. (2014, May). *Segregating California's future: Inequality and its alternative 60 years after Brown v. Board of Education.* Los Angeles: UCLA, The Civil Rights Project/Proyecto Derechos Civiles.

CHAPTER SIX

Immigration and Language Policies in California Education

Guiding Questions

1. *What has been the trend in the United States regarding education for students of recently immigrated families?*
2. *What is the transnational model of immigration?*
3. *What are several models of education for English Learners within California?*

Introduction

The history of immigration to the United States and California is one filled with an ebb and flow of immigrants from different regions of the world. At the same time, U.S. and California policies toward immigration have been full of attempts to codify who counts as a legal immigrant, an accepted refugee, or an undocumented resident of the United States. Californians have also changed their views on immigration over time. According to a study by the Public Policy Institute of California (Bonner, 2019), fewer than 50% of Californians in 1998 believed that immigrants are a "benefit" to the state of California. By 2018, that percentage rose to 72%. This sets the tone for how immigration and English Language educational laws have also changed over time in California. This chapter will begin by describing immigrant and refugee patterns in California, then will discuss U.S. and California education laws over time as a reflection of immigration patterns. It will also provide readers with a greater awareness of the support systems—including organizations and associations—that will enable them to become involved in improving education for English Language learners as well as recent immigrants to California.

Immigration Patterns

California, and the United States as a whole, has experienced several different types of immigration patterns. Chinese laborers originally immigrated to California to engage in labor positions such as mining and railroad construction, but faced legal discrimination on their way to establishing a familial and cultural presence in the state (see Chapter One for further discussion). This chapter will discuss patterns of immigration in the twentieth century, noting the trends in immigrant movements and U.S. and state policies regarding the education of children of immigrant families.

Japanese Immigration

Japanese immigrants to the United States came to Hawaii and California in the late 1800s, finding work in agriculture, as domestic helpers, and as small business owners. Beginning as tenant farmers, Japanese immigrants worked very successfully in California's agricultural valley, buying land and setting up farms. By 1920, Japanese farmers owned and worked on more than 50% of California's vegetable-growing farmland. However, in the early 1900s, a series of increasingly restrictive bills were passed, limiting the number of immigrants from Japan. First, in 1907, President Theodore Roosevelt signed the Gentlemen's Agreement between the United States and Japan. Under the terms of the agreement, if Japan would stop issuing exit visas to Japanese laborers, then those Japanese already in the United States would be allowed to bring their families to the United States. Following this informal agreement, which greatly reduced the numbers of Japanese immigrants to the United States, California passed additional restriction acts that made it illegal for the Japanese to own land. In what was called the California Alien Land Bill of 1913, Japanese immigrants were barred from owning or leasing land because of their noncitizen standing. To avoid being restricted by such laws, many Japanese Issei (first generation to have arrived in the United States) purchased and leased lands in their children's names (Nisei, who were born in the United States). As citizens, the Nisei children should have been legally allowed to own and work on the land. However, the 1920 passage of the Alien Land Bill denied the Japanese Americans even that right.

For resources about education during the internment of Japanese and Japanese Americans in camps during WWII, when 30,000 people were forced into "relocation" camps in seven states, including two in California—Manzanar and Tule Lake—*see Figure 6.1.*

FIGURE 6.1 - SELECTED RESOURCES ON EDUCATION IN JAPANESE INTERNMENT CAMPS

Selected Archival Collections Online

- Letters from the Japanese American Internment, Smithsonian Education online, http://www.smithsonianeducation.org/educators/lesson_plans/japanese_internment/home_away.html
- Uprooted! Japanese Americans During WWII, California Museum, http://www.californiamuseum.org/uprooted-japanese-americans-during-wwii
- Japanese American Archival Collection, California State University, Sacramento, https://library.csus.edu/japanese-american-archival-collection
- Denshō, a grass roots organization dedicated to preserving, educating, and sharing information about Japanese internment, with an online education center, http://densho.org/

Mexican Immigration

Mexicans have a unique relationship with what is now California (the term Mexicans will be used here to account for Mexican citizens and Mexican Americans). While they have lived in the territory for hundreds of years, and were able to claim it as part of the Mexican nation with their independence from Spain in 1821, they are also recent immigrants to what is now the United States. They have faced a dizzying array of policies that range from being welcomed, to being turned away, to being "repatriated" (deported) to their former country. From unrestricted immigration, to the encouragement of immigration for use for field labor, to restrictions on immigration, to the actual physical removal of Mexicans and Mexican Americans, the policies of the United States toward Mexican immigration have been highly inconsistent (Noel, 2018). For example, in 1924, the U.S. Congress established the Border Patrol to monitor movement across the Mexico–U.S. border. This border had previously been open to free movement back and forth, but with the establishment of the Border Patrol, the United States created an immigration policy that physically limited the number of Mexicans who could enter the country. From 1929 to 1934, the United States "repatriated" more than 400,000 Mexicans, of which approximately 200,000 had been born in the United States and thus were U.S. citizens. This means that the United States illegally forced out its own citizens, based solely on their nationality. Of those who were deported, 64,000 were forced to move to Mexico without any legal proceedings.

But the inconsistent nature of U.S. policies regarding Mexican immigration shifted toward encouraging more immigration, this time in 1942, when the U.S. and Mexican governments signed an agreement to intentionally bring Mexicans to the United States through the "Bracero Program." The agreement authorized a number of Mexican immigrants to work temporarily in the United States in jobs such as seasonal agricultural work. This was undertaken, in part, to fill the labor needs of the United States due to the loss of workers during World War II. Under this new program, the United States offered protection of workers for the time that they were in the country, but then the workers were required to return to Mexico.

Transnational Immigration

Today, some immigrant families are considered to be "transnational," crossing back and forth between their original country and the United States in order to maintain and strengthen family, community, cultural, and economic ties. Family members often live in multiple countries, due to the necessity of moving to and through countries during the immigration process. As an example, a high school student in a study by Pandya, Pagdilao, Kim, and Marquez (2015) explains: "My sister was born in El Salvador and my two *tios* were born in SoCal. I have family in Moreno Valley [outside of Los Angeles], in Tecate [on both sides of the border between California and Mexico], and close to my house. I also have sisters in El Salvador" (p. 15).

While in many cases families engage in the act of "border crossing," physically traveling back and forth between countries, a new form of transnationalism through technology has developed in recent years. As Portes and Rumbaut (2014) explain,

> Immigrants today can keep themselves informed, on a daily basis, of events in their home communities and countries . . . They can call their families every day, regardless of distance, and send electronic mail to them, as well as to community leaders and government authorities. (p. 173)

In this way, families across country lines can keep abreast of important family events, while also participating in the civil engagement of each country if they so choose.

Deferred Action for Childhood Arrivals (DACA)

For youth who arrived in the United States with their families and face potential deportation once they reach adulthood (at least in the current national climate), the Deferred Action for Childhood Arrivals (DACA) has been a critical option. Signed by then-President Obama in 2012, DACA allows individuals to submit applications to defer any detention or deportation action based on their immigrant status. Those who qualify receive a two-year exemption from detention or deportation, as long as they follow all laws. In addition to several additional requirements, candidates can be considered for DACA status if (a) they came to the United States prior to turning 16 years old, (b) lived continuously in the United States from 2007 to the present, and (c) were under the age of 31 in 2012. Under these conditions, there were 200,150 persons with DACA status in California as of August 2018 (Migration Policy Institute, 2018).

Refugees

Another type of movement to the United States is the immigrant who comes to this country requesting asylum under refugee status. To gain acceptance as a refugee in the United States, a person must fit a specific description. The definition of a refugee used by the United States is someone from outside the

United States whose country is of special humanitarian concern to the United States, who can demonstrate that they were persecuted or lived in fear of persecution due to race, religion, nationality, and political opinion, and who is not firmly resettled in another country (U.S. Citizenship and Immigrant Services).

In the early part of the twenty-first century, humanitarian crises around the world have raised the level of awareness of the situation of refugees. According to the U.S. State Department's Worldwide Refugee Admissions Processing data, 84,994 refugees were admitted to the United States in 2016. The leading countries of nationality for refugee requests in 2016 were the Democratic Republic of the Congo, Syria, Myanmar, Iraq, and Somalia, with these five countries comprising 71% of all admitted refugees. Refugees from countries next most often requesting asylum include Bhutan, Iran, Afghanistan, Ukraine, and Eritea. In total, these 10 countries comprise 91% of all refugees admitted to the United States in 2016. These numbers will undoubtedly change, depending on the status of the "travel ban" that President Trump ordered. The travel ban blocked entry to the United States from six countries for a period of 90 days, until further notice: Iran, Somalia, Sudan, Yemen, Syria, and Libya.

National Immigration Policy

The number of immigrants legally allowed into the United States each year has varied over time, as have the categories of immigrants that have been allowed. From the 1920s to the 1990s, immigration policies were highly based on regions, but began to move away from nationality and in addition to deal with refugee and asylum policies. The National Origins Act of 1924 set the ceiling for immigration at 164,667 new immigrants each year. After World War II, the U.S. government began to allow immigrants and refugees from selected countries to enter the country under special compensation. The Displaced Persons Act of 1948 provided for 100,000 "displaced persons" to enter each year, giving priority to those who had been displaced by the war. By 1951, the act was amended to allow 400,000 persons into the United States under this special clause. Then in 1952, for the first time, some of the nationality-based provisions were rescinded, while others were continued. For instance, the Japanese exclusion was repealed, and Asian nations were allowed small increases in quotas of immigrants. However, this act, the McCarran-Walter Immigration and Nationality Act, also maintained the general idea of a national origins quota system, still limiting immigration to a certain number based on nationality. In addition, this act described the type of person that could not enter the United States, barring "radicals, communists, and subversives" from entering the country (Noel, 2018). Not until the Immigration Act of 1965 was the concept of restricting immigration based on national origin abolished (on a temporary basis). This act set different immigration ceilings from Western and Eastern Hemisphere immigrants. For the Western Hemisphere, the number of immigrants that could enter the United States was set at 120,000, whereas for the Eastern Hemisphere, the number was 170,000. But again making the practice of immigration and immigration policy more complicated, those from the Eastern Hemisphere were admitted based on a preference scale, with immigrants who had either family ties or occupational skills needed by the United States being given rights of entry. Immigration policy was changed again, this time in 1978, when the rate of immigration was finally not tied to region but rather was looked at as worldwide, and the ceiling for immigrants was set at 290,000.

The trend over the past 20 years has been to pass federal laws aimed at increasing the number of ways that immigrants can be deported from the United States, or to keep out immigrants from certain countries. The Department of Homeland Security was formed in 2002, which enacts surveillance and oversees the U.S. Citizenship and Immigration Services, the U.S. Customs and Border Protection, and the U.S. Immigration and Customs Enforcement agencies. The fact that immigration is placed mainly under Homeland Security demonstrates the level of concern that immigration needs to be under a "security" agency. In 2006 the U.S. Congress passed the "Secure Fence Act," mandating the construction of over 700 miles of fence along the U.S.-Mexican border. This act is being addressed again with President Trump's Executive Order to instead build a wall along the 700-mile border.

Current California Immigration Trends

According to the U.S. Census Bureau, in 2017 California had a population of over 39 million residents. This number is assuredly smaller than reality, as it does not count people who are experiencing homelessness and does not always accurately count the number of recent immigrants. Of this population, slightly over 25% are people who were born in other countries. Looking at these numbers more closely, 50% of recent immigrants come from Latin America (including Mexico and the countries in Central and South America), 39.7% come from the many countries and regions that make up Asia, and 6.4% come from Europe. More specifically, California has the highest populations of several immigrant or refugee groups in the country.

- Hmong—With over 100,000 Hmong residents, California has the highest number of Hmong of any state in the United States, especially in the central valley area. Fresno, Sacramento, Merced, and Stockton are in the top six cities nationally for number of Hmong. Several Hmong-focused schools have opened in these cities, and there is a Hmong bilingual teaching authorization designed for teachers who want to teach Hmong in the schools.

- Vietnamese—California is home to the largest number of Vietnamese of any state in the United States as well. Los Angeles is home to approximately 240,000 Vietnamese, followed by the San Jose area with just over 100,000. San Francisco, Oakland, and San Diego are also in the top eight cities with large numbers of Vietnamese in the United States.

- Iraq, Iran, and Middle Easterners—According to the California Department of Social Services, more than 36,000 refugees resettled in California between 2011 and 2016. While the counties with the largest refugee populations are, in order: San Diego, Los Angeles, Sacramento, Orange, and Santa Clara, refugees live in 31 of California's 56 counties.

- Mexican/Mexican American—California and Los Angeles have the largest population of any state and any city in the United States.

- California is also home to large numbers of Filipinos, Central Americans—especially El Salvadorans and Guatemalans, Pacific Islanders, and European Americans—Bulgarian, Hungarian, Romanian, Russian, as well as other countries.

California Education for Children of Immigrant Families

"The immigration status of students in California has been the subject of a variety of laws and legal challenges. Current law states that school-age children who reside in California must not be denied a free public education based on citizenship status" (CDE, 2018, November 27, https://www.cde.ca.gov/re/lr/cl/cefistatus.asp). How did California get to this current law requiring that all children receive a free public education, regardless of citizenship status? *Brown v Board of Education* in 1954 is widely seen as the critical turning point in desegregating schools. However, California's role in the development of desegregation is often overlooked. In particular, *Alvarez v Lemon Grove* (1931) and *Mendez v Westminster* (1946) were early precursors to the national desegregation efforts.

Education for Mexican and Mexican American Children

California state educational law did not designate Mexican or Mexican-American children as a distinct group from Whites, as it did with Blacks, Chinese, and Native Americans. By 1927, while California state law no longer allowed educational segregation of Black children, new language allowed the state to establish separate schools for Chinese, Japanese, Mongolian, or "Indian" children (1927, Political Code section 1662). This meant that Mexican children could legally attend regular public schools as "White" children. (The term "Mexican" here is used purposely, although the children were of Latinx descent and 95% were American. The purpose of using the term Mexican in this section is to reinforce the decisions to segregate children into "Mexican schools" or "Mexican rooms.") This did not, however, mean that school districts followed the law. Efforts to segregate Mexican children were seen in the creation of separate schools—called "Mexican Schools"—and were most often attempted to be justified by the need for separate education due to language differences. Two court cases in particular led to changes in state law barring segregation based on race, ethnicity, or language.

Roberto Alvarez v Board of Trustees of the Lemon Grove School District (1931)

One such case of a school district attempting to segregate Mexican children came in 1930–1931 in Lemon Grove, in San Diego County, in the case of *Roberto Alvarez v Board of Trustees of the Lemon Grove School District* (1931), commonly known as "The Lemon Grove Incident" (Alvarez, 1986; Madrid, 2008). After having an integrated school for White and Mexican students, the district decided to build a separate school for its over 70 Mexican students. Children were then not allowed to enter the regular public school, being told, instead, to attend the separate school, which was a barn-like structure that became known as the "caballeriza," a place for horses. School district officials believed that a separate school needed to be built in order to "Americanize" the Mexican children, mainly to teach them American customs and to speak English. Trustees used language such as "backward" and "deficient" to describe the Mexican children. The new school was situated in the "Mexican part of town," and school district officials described this placement as being a safety issue. Parents of the Mexican children refused to send their children to the separate school, so only three children attended the new "Mexican School." Despite the fact that the segregation decision was supported by the Lemon Grove Chamber of Commerce and the all-White Parent Teacher Association, the parents of the Mexican students began to organize in order to fight the decision. They formed neighborhood groups, found legal counsel, and publicized the incident in major English and Spanish language newspapers. This came at great risk, as it has been reported that several parents were deported to Mexico because of these efforts.

This case involved issues of national origin and ethnic identity. The lawsuit pointed out that 95% of the Mexican students were born in the United States, and thus were citizens of the United States. Further, it was shown as evidence through the trial that some Mexican children lived in the White part of town, and some Whites lived in the Mexican part of town, thus invalidating the "safety" reason for placing the school in the mostly segregated neighborhood.

Judge Chambers ruled in favor of the families and ordered that the children be immediately allowed to attend the regular Lemon Grove Grammar School, as they had prior to the attempted segregation. Unfortunately, this victory was only seen at the local level, as it did not address the entire state of California.

Mendez v Westminster (1946–1947)

The *Mendez et al. v Westminster School District of Orange County, et al.*, was filed in 1946 and decided in 1947. It addressed the same sort of problems raised in the *Alverez v Lemon Grove* case—the establishment of segregated schools for Mexican children. Once the family had won their case, the school district appealed their case to the California Court of Appeals, but lost the case there as well. At issue was that segregated "Mexican Schools" violated state law that did not allow segregation of Mexican children (Moll, 2010).

The Mendez family, along with four other families, argued that the separate schools for the 5,000 "Mexican" children in Orange County were illegal, based on the fact that Mexicans were considered White. The school district had used language differences as the reason to segregate children into Mexican schools, but in this case added skin complexion and last name as contributing factors. They argued that some of the Mexican children had last names that sounded too "Mexican" or were too dark-skinned to attend school with White children, even offering to allow one lighter-skinned Mexican child the opportunity to continue in the White school (Moll, 2010). In attempting to negotiate a solution before the case went to trial, the school district offered Gonzalo and Felicitas Mendez the opportunity to allow their children to continue to attend the regular school with the White children. However, in an effort to help the entire Mexican community, the Mendezes declined and took the case to court. As the family had gained some financial resources through first opening a restaurant and then leasing and running a farm that employed 30 workers, they agreed to help fund the case.

González (1999) describes that "Nothing appeared to indicate that segregated schooling required modification, and it remained the prescription of choice for "remedying" Mexican culture (p. 71). The impact on children was a key point in this case, as it was in the later *Brown v Board of Education* case. Moll (2010) explains that in the testimonies of educational experts who spoke at the trial, "Two main themes prevailed in their testimonies: (a) how segregation fosters harmful feelings of inferiority and rejection in children, and (b) how isolation delays acculturation (Americanization) and English language learning" (p. 452).

Moll (2010) describes the significance of the Mendez case:

> Thus did Gonzalo and Felicita Méndez—a Mexican and a Puerto Rican, immigrants, bilinguals and U.S. citizens, parents and community members, agricultural laborers, business owners, tenant farmers, and champions of children, with the help of neighbors, institutions, and organizations representing different races and ethnicities—help change the history of education in this country. It was the beginning of the end of mandated racially segregated schools in California and elsewhere, a process of change that would become national in scope and ratified legally through the Brown case. (p. 454)

Court Cases Related to Education for Immigrant Students—1970s to the Present

Even though the right to an education within California had been gained, the struggles continue through to today, with shifting national and state climate regarding education based on citizenship or immigrant status. Some of the key legislation is described next.

Graham v Richardson

A U.S. Supreme Court case in 1971, *Graham v. Richardson,* set the tone for treatment of undocumented immigrants by deciding "that aliens could not be denied welfare benefits simply on the basis that they were aliens" (Fisher, 1995, p. 22).

Plyler v Doe

A crucial case in 1982 continued this path of allowing rights to all U.S. residents. In the Texas case *Plyler v. Doe,* "the Supreme Court ruled that undocumented children cannot be denied access to education solely on the basis of their immigration status" (Lucas, 1997, p. 7). The court in this case further elaborated on their decision by finding that "children of people who came to this country illegally cannot be denied the same free public education available to other children. The Court expressed that it was especially concerned that these children would be forever 'second-class citizens' without an education" (Fisher, 1995, p. A-4). It is important to note the deliberate use of the word people in this case. The point here is that the U.S. Constitution protects people, not only those designated citizens. The history of this case was that noncitizens were required by the state of Texas to pay for public school or not be allowed to go to school. This requirement barred about 50 children of noncitizen residents from attending school because they could not afford to pay the tuition. The U.S. Supreme Court felt that without being able to receive an education these children would be forever harmed.

On September 27, 1981, the California State Board of Education (SBE) filed an *amicus curiae* brief with the U.S. Supreme Court in the case of *Plyler v. Doe,* 457 US 202 (1982), which is basically an argument supporting the families. In arguing against Texas statutes that denied public school enrollment and withheld state funds from local school districts for children "illegally admitted" to the United States, the SBE stated:

> As educators concerned with the provision of quality education for all children and for the improvement of society through an educated population, the California State Board of Education believes strongly that there is no rational educational or fiscal purpose in excluding children of illegal aliens from receiving the educational opportunities available to all other children. (https://www.cde.ca.gov/re/lr/cl/cefistatus.asp)

However, this sentiment in California was to change by 1994.

Proposition 187

Anti-immigrant sentiment arose again with the passage of Proposition 187 (Prop 187) in 1994 in California, which denied noncitizens the rights of daily life in California. Prop 187 prohibited illegal immigrants (what we now call undocumented immigrants) from attending any public school at any level and required that school administrators and teachers were to report to the government any students or parents that they suspected of being illegal. This proposition also denied nonemergency medical care and childhood vaccinations. In addition, it prohibited all illegal immigrants from receiving any funding for social services. Ultimately, the federal courts struck down Prop 187, because it was in violation of federal immigration law, and in 2014 California passed into law SB-396, which nullified all portions of Prop 187 that were in conflict with the U.S. Constitution and other federal law.

Laws and Court Cases Related to Language Policies in Education

Almost half of public school students in California live in homes where the most frequently spoken language is not English. Of those, about half are designated as English Learners by their school districts based on their home language, state test scores, and other criteria. California has long been home to the largest number of English Learners in the United States, with approximately 1.5 million in 2017, comprising nearly a quarter of the state's students. Although California's ELs speak over 65 different languages, the vast majority speak Spanish as their primary language.

Bilingual Education in California provides an education in the student's home language while the student attends school to learn English (CDE, 2018). By far the most common approach is to teach English Learners in the same classroom as monolingual English speakers. However, two models of Bilingual Education are being practiced more commonly in California today. In the 90:10 approach, students spend 90% of their day in a classroom taught in a language other than English (including Spanish, Hmong, and others). Then 10% of their day is with the regular classroom. Students are reevaluated each year by the English Language Proficiency Assessments for California (ELPAC—see Chapter Five for further discussion), and as they move toward English language proficiency, they are placed back into the regular classroom. A second model is the 50:50, where half of a student's school day is instructed in English and the other in a second language. While this serves English Learners, students who are monolingual English speakers also have the opportunity to participate in this model, to become bilingual.

Bilingual Education Act, 1968

As part of the evolving Elementary and Secondary Education Act, first signed in 1965, Title VII, the Bilingual Education Act of 1968, required that for programs receiving funding for bilingual education in K-12 schools, funding would be provided for the development of new programs, training of teachers, and long-term maintenance of such programs.

Lau v Nichols, 1974

In a case brought by the Lau family of San Francisco but eventually argued at the U.S. Supreme Court level, the family argued that their Chinese American children, who were in regular public classrooms, were not being given the support needed to succeed in school due to their lack of proficiency with the English language. They were, in essence, left to "sink or swim" in schools that did not acknowledge the needs of English Language Learners. In ruling in favor of the family, the U.S. Supreme Court acknowledged that English Learners need additional support in schools. Following this landmark decision, the U.S. Department of Education put into place the "Lau Remedies," a set of recommended practices to support bilingual learners, including identifying and evaluating English language capacity in learners, determining effective instructional strategies, and determining when bilingual students could learn properly in an English-only classroom. Importantly, these laws and remedies did not require bilingual education programs, but allowed schools to determine which method to use to teach English Learners to speak English.

AB-1329, Chacon-Moscone Bilingual-Bicultural Act of 1976

This was the first California law that mandated school districts to provide English Learners with specifically bilingual education programs. This lasted until 1987, when the bill was allowed to "sunset," or be taken off the records. However, this law at least provided the start to bilingual programs around the state, and many districts continued in these efforts. The California Department of Education during this time frame made several changes to more clearly identify how schools should identify and teach their English Learners.

Proposition 227 ("Prop 227"), 1998, the English Language in Public Schools Act

Aligning with a timeframe of anti-immigrant sentiment in California, which included the 1994 passage of Prop 187 that denied immigrants services, in 1998 voters passed Prop 227, the English Language in Public Schools Act. This Act required that all students be taught only in English, in English-only classrooms, after giving English Learners one year to learn English. This outlawed bilingual education.

Proposition 58 ("Prop 58"), the California Multilingual Education Act

Prop 58 authorizes California school districts to establish dual-language immersion programs. Approved by a 73.5% yes vote by California voters, the law went into effect July 1, 2017. This law served to overturn previous anti-bilingual education legislation and now authorizes schools to provide bilingual education, including the 90:10 and 50:50 models described earlier, also called dual-immersion, due to the students being immersed into two different languages.

Organizations Related to Immigration and Bilingual Education

California has developed countless organizations to assist those who have immigrated to the state. Some of these are official government agencies, some are community organizations, and some are academic organizations. This section will focus on organizations and on school-community partnerships, giving just a few examples to represent the work of many valuable organizations.

California Association of Bilingual Education (CABE)

CABE is a nonprofit organization established in 1976 to advocate for and instruct educators for bilingual education and quality educational experiences for all students in California. "CABE recognizes and honors the fact that we live in a rich multicultural, global society and that respect for diversity makes us a stronger state and nation" (http://www.gocabe.org/index.php/about/about-cabe/). CABE hosts an annual conference for educators to keep up on bilingual education practices, has regional chapters, professional development opportunities, and provides resources for educators teaching English Learners.

National Association of Multicultural Education (NAME), California Chapter

NAME is a national organization whose mission is "Advancing and Advocating for Social Justice & Equality" (https://www.nameorg.org/index.php). Operating since 1990, NAME provides annual conferences, resources and teaching materials, a multicultural education journal, and many other forms of communication to help educators keep up with the field. The California Chapter of NAME has recently focused on Ethnic Studies, providing teaching materials and other resources for educators. Their 2019 conference was titled "Teaching in the Face of (Im)Migration, Incarceration, and Borders: Ethnic Studies Resistance."

School Districts with Community Partnerships for Immigrant and Dreamer Students

With a shifting federal climate that has discouraged or banned immigration, and with the threat of deportation hovering for hundreds of thousands of U.S. residents, many California school districts have made clear their support for DACA, Dreamer, and immigrant students and their families. Two examples will illustrate how school districts can partner with their communities to provide support and guidance for their students' families. Both districts recognize that immigration status is a matter of urgency not only for their students, but especially for their families, and have created their own centers as well as partnered with immigrant support organizations and legal aid centers in their communities to provide safe spaces for families to address immigration issues.

San José Unified School District (SJUSD). SJUSD provides a full section on their website of Immigration Resources. The district proclaims very clearly that

> San José Unified welcomes all students, regardless of their immigration status. However, many of our students and families are experiencing anxiety and uncertainty as a result of some of the proposed policy changes at the federal level. With that in mind, the Board of Education passed a resolution on February 9, 2017, supporting immigrant students and families. https://web.sjusd.org/your-resources/community-resources

With this visible level of support, the district then provides a list and links to immigration legal services such as La Raza Centro Legal and Asian Pacific Islander Legal Outreach. SJUSD also provides updates on DACA status and resources, and has partnered with Santa Clara County to provide a "Santa Clara County Toolkit for School Districts to Support Immigrant Students & Their Families" (https://sjusd.app.box.com/s/74y4096bn5pwjhvfxrqa624ynmcw35r3).

Fresno Unified School District. Fresno Unified also provides visible support for immigrant students and their families through their Dream Resource Center. "Fresno Unified is committed to supporting our DACA students and staff. The Dream Resource Center will provide instrumental help by adequately supporting our immigrant students, staff and their families" (https://www.fresnounified.org/schools/fas/Pages/Dream-Resource-Center.aspx). The Dream Resource Center offers classes such as "Know Your Rights" and "Citizenship Pre-Screening," and provides the full range of Student Services, Community Resources, and Immigrant Integration to assist families dealing with threats to their residency in the United States.

Issues of Equity and Social Justice

The entire history of education based on citizenship or immigration status in California has been one of an ongoing policy and voter statements regarding immigrant rights to education, infringement on rights, and outright denial of rights to an education.

Reflective and Action-Based Questions

1. *Describe four U.S. immigration laws over time that have impacted Mexican immigrants.*
2. *Discuss the trends regarding bilingual education since the 1960s.*
3. *Do some research and find out the different ethnicities of groups of people who have lived in your community throughout history. Has any particular group moved in and then moved out over time? Have certain groups held certain positions in your community more than others? Can you trace the current practices or institutions within your community that began with the traditions of a particular group?*
4. *Reflect on what would be required for new immigrants to fit into either your community or your school. What resources are available within your community or your school that would be helpful for people new to the community? Prepare a guide for possible new immigrants to your community or your school, listing and describing the information and resources that are available for their use if needed.*

References

Alvarez, Jr., R. (1986). The Lemon Grove Incident: The nation's first successful desegregation court case. *The Journal of San Diego History, 32*(2), 116–135.

Bonner, D. (2019, March 20). *Californians' views of immigration policy—Now and then.* San Francisco: Public Policy Institute of California.

California Department of Education. (2018). *California English Learner Roadmap: Strengthening comprehensive educational policies, programs, and practices for English Learners.* Sacramento: Author.

California Department of Education. (2018, November 27). *Immigration status of students—CalEdFacts.* Retrieved from https://www.cde.ca.gov/re/lr/cl/cefistatus.asp

Fisher, M. (1995). *Equal protection under law: Access to public education.* Washington, DC: Office of Juvenile Justice and Delinquent Prevention.

González, G. (1999). Segregation and the education of Mexican children, 1900–1940. In J. Moreno (Ed.), *The elusive quest for equality: 150 years of Chicano/Chicana education* (pp. 53–76). Cambridge, MA: Harvard Educational Review Reprint Series No. 32.

Lucas, T. (1997). *Influences on the educational experiences of immigrant students to U.S. schools.* New Jersey: Author.

Madrid, E. M. (2008). The unheralded history of the Lemon Grove desegregation case. *Multicultural Education, 15*(3), 15–19.

Migration Policy Institute. (2018, August). *Deferred Action for Childhood Arrivals (DACA) data tools.* Retrieved from https://www.migrationpolicy.org/programs/data-hub/deferred-action-childhood-arrivals-daca-profiles

Moll, L. C. (2010). Mobilizing culture, language, and educational practices: Fulfilling the promises of Mendez and Brown. *Educational Researcher, 39*(6), 451–460.

Noel, J. (2018). *Developing multicultural educators* (3rd ed.). Long Grove, IL: Waveland Press, Inc.

Pandya, J. Z., Pagdilao, K. C., Kim, A. E., & Marquez, E. (2015). Transnational children orchestrating competing voices in multimodal, digital autobiographies. *Teachers College Record, 117*(7), 1–32.

Portes, A., & Rumbaut, R. G. (2014). *Immigrant America: A portrait* (4th ed.). Berkeley: University of California Press.

CHAPTER SEVEN

Family and Community Engagement

Guiding Questions

1. *What types of support for family engagement are offered by the federal, state, district, and schools?*
2. *What types of opportunities are available for teachers to become involved in their school's surrounding community?*
3. *How does California's Local Control Accountability Plan ensure that families and communities are involved in school planning?*

Introduction

Education does not occur in a vacuum in a classroom or in a school; the school is set within the context of its community. In order for schools to have the best opportunity to educate their students, a large array of community-based organizations, public agencies, nonprofit organizations, parent groups, and businesses provide services that enable a more complete education than can be offered by the school alone. Teachers and future teachers can enhance their own relationships with their students by learning about, and becoming involved with, both the families and the community organizations. By building these relationships, parents and communities can enhance student learning, and schools can help enhance the families and communities they serve. This chapter lays out family engagement policies and practices at the federal, state, district, and school levels. This discussion will by no means be complete, but rather will introduce readers to the wide variety of types of family and community involvement that is available.

Federal Focus on Family and Community Engagement

The U.S. Department of Education has long provided a focus on family and community engagement, through policy, practice, support, and best practice recommendations.

Federal Policy

Within the current Every Student Succeeds Act (ESSA) of 2015 is laid out "Section 1116. Parent and Family Engagement." Of critical importance in the policy is the requirement that schools and districts engage with parents and families to jointly develop the plans and policies for parent involvement. *Components of the policy on Parent and Family Engagement can be seen in Figure 7.1.*

FIGURE 7.1 - PARENT AND FAMILY ENGAGEMENT IN THE EVERY STUDENT SUCCEEDS ACT

(a) Local Education Agencies (LEAs)—will receive funding on the condition that they provide meaningful involvement activities for parents and families

(b) School parent and family engagement policy—must be jointly developed between LEAs/schools and parents, and this policy must be written in order to provide clarity and consistency

(c) Policy involvement—through meetings that are made accessible to all parents

(d) Shared responsibility for high student academic achievement—through a jointly prepared compact to be signed by LEAs/schools and parents to express their roles in sharing this responsibility

(e) Building capacity for involvement—LEAs/schools must provide materials and training for parents to better understand how they can be involved in their child's education

(f) Accessibility—LEAs/schools must carry out the parent and family engagement activities in ways that are accessible to parents who have limited English proficiency, family members who have disabilities, and migrant families

(g) Family engagement in education programs—LEAs/schools must develop parent education programs and must inform parents of the availability of those programs

(h) Review—each state will review the actions of its districts and schools to ensure that each of these requirements are met (summarized from https://www.esc16.net/upload/page/0367/PublicLaw%20.pdf)

U.S. Department of Education Support

There are numerous forms of support for parent, family, and community engagement. Some are organizations formed through the private sector, others are found in various agencies of the U.S. government. The U.S. Department of Health & Human Services, for example, funds a number of community engagement programs such as the Out-of-School Time and Community Program, which connects communities with after-school programs. The U.S. Department of Housing and Urban Development provides guidance to community developers on neighborhood schools and how to engage with parents.

For its part, the U.S. Department of Education has established "The Family and Community Engagement Team," with the goal of expanding the U.S. Department of Education's efforts "to help schools, districts, and states better engage in education. The Team is committed to supporting parents and families by empowering them and giving them a voice and an opportunity to be engaged. The team strives to be inclusive of multiple groups and perspectives, with members from the Office for Civil Rights, Office of Special Education and Rehabilitative Services, Center for Faith Based and Neighborhood Partnership, and Office of English Language Acquisition, among other representatives, all for the purpose of ensuring that the team provides support for many groups within society. The Family and Community Engagement Team provides information and support, but also listening and collaborating sessions, through many channels, including parent forums, webinars, tweets, texts, and roundtables, all of which provide information to and receive information from families about cultural and local concerns. The effort is to support families and communities by both providing updated information and learning about local needs of families and communities.

Finally, community engagement is also an important part of education at the federal, state, district, and school levels. Community engagement can be seen in both policy and recommendations of best practices, and refers to both the community becoming engaged in a school's efforts to educate its students and to the school becoming an integral part of its surrounding community. The ESSA includes policies on many forms of community engagement. In describing physical spaces where schools and communities can work together, there are "21st Century Community Learning Centers" and "Full Service Community Schools." ESSA also includes a policy requiring schools to coordinate with community organizations, social service agencies, local businesses, and workforce development organizations to help not only students but their families as well. As can be seen, then, federal policy values both parents/families and communities as essential partners in the education of K-12 students.

California Focus Family and Community Engagement

Similar to the federal focus on families and community engagement, the California Department of Education, along with the Education Code, provides both policy and support for families and communities to be engaged with the educational process.

California Policy and Programs

California educational policy is codified in the Education Code (see Chapter Two and Appendix A). Often, these policies are the result of either federal or state legislation. The California Education Code 11500-11506 requires that districts establish "Programs to Encourage Parental Involvement" (*see Figure 7.2 on page 101*), many of which will be discussed in the remainder of this chapter. It is left to the districts and schools to make decisions about which types of parent involvement programs would be most effective based on their communities and their demographics. Occasionally, though, California voters pass a state-wide proposition related to parent involvement, and often state legislators pass bills that the governor then signs. The Education Code provides the legislation for these efforts, and sometimes a program is slated to receive funding. While the funding for these types of programs does not always last into perpetuity, they provide examples of what is important in terms of family and community engagement within California.

Support for Parents/Families and Communities

The California Department of Education provides a number of explanatory guides, videos, and other similarly informative materials for parents, families, and community members to better understand the educational system and to learn best practices.

Figure 7.2 - Parental Involvement in the Education Code

Education Code

CHAPTER 16. Programs to Encourage Parental Involvement

11501.
It is the intent of the Legislature in enacting this chapter to ensure that parent and family engagement programs are properly designed and implemented and to provide a focus and structure for these programs based on prior experience and research while maintaining sufficient local flexibility to design a program that best meets the needs of the local community.

11502.
It is the purpose and goal of this chapter to do all of the following:

(a) To engage parents and family members positively in their children's education by providing assistance and training on topics such as state academic standards and assessments to develop knowledge and skills to use at home to support their children's academic efforts at school and their children's development as responsible future members of our society.

(b) To inform parents that they can directly affect the success of their children's learning, by providing parents with techniques and strategies that they may utilize to improve their children's academic success and to assist their children in learning at home.

(c) To build consistent and effective two-way communication between family members and the school so that parents and family members may know when and how to assist their children in support of classroom learning activities.

(d) To train teachers, school administrators, specialized instructional support personnel, and other staff to communicate effectively with parents as equal partners.

(e) To integrate and coordinate parent and family engagement activities with the local control and accountability plan adopted pursuant to Section 47606.5, 52060, or 52066, as applicable, with other programs.

Centers for Families of Children with Disabilities. One area of family engagement that the CDE has helped facilitate is centers to provide information and resources for families of children with disabilities. These centers help families understand the complexity of the Individuals with Disabilities Act (IDEA), providing information and resources to help parents help their children through the educational system.

Parent Training and Information Centers. Multiple centers throughout the state, funded by the U.S. Department of Education. These centers provide workshops and training on parent rights and responsibilities, how to meet educational goals, and information packets, while providing support groups and individual parent support.

California Community Parent Resource Centers (CPRC). CPRCs have the purpose of ensuring that parents of children with disabilities have training and information to help their children, specifically parents that are themselves underserved such as those with disabilities, low income, or limited English proficiency. This is also based on federal policy.

Family Empowerment Centers. The establishment of Family Empowerment Centers is specifically a California creation, being created by Senate Bill 511 and Education Code 5600-56414. These centers are established so that parents, guardians, and families of children and young adults with disabilities have information, training, and support to help meet the needs of their children. There is currently funding allocated through SB 511 for each center.

Family Engagement Toolkit. The CDE has also designed a document to help districts and schools create stronger school-family connections called the "Family Engagement Toolkit." This document describes the importance of strong school-family connections, lays out best practices, and provides six tools to help create a stronger connection, especially emphasizing the importance of including the families and perspectives of the diversity represented within the district.

TOOL 1. Establish a district family engagement team

Have we identified prospective parent leaders from all of our communities?
Does the list of prospective team members reflect the diversity of our district?

TOOL 2. Create a vision statement for family engagement

Will this vision statement resonate with families of all student groups?
Does this vision statement include a role for all stakeholders?
Will this vision statement serve as an inspiration for all stakeholders?

TOOL 3. Identify current level of trust between educators and families

How welcome do our families feel at our school/district?
Are there differences between different groups of families, by grade levels or schools?

TOOL 4. Identify current levels of connections to student learning in family engagement efforts

Do district plans include family engagement actions as part of each student learning goal?
How confident do educators feel about partnering with families to support student learning?
Do families understand effective ways to support their child's learning?

TOOL 5. Review existing family engagement activities

How well does each activity contribute to building trusting relationships?
How well does each activity connect family engagement to student learning?

TOOL 6. Plan to strengthen trusting relationships

Do families feel welcome and trusting of educators and staff?

TOOL 7. Plan to strengthen connections to student learning

Identify goals, objectives, activities, and progress indicators.

TOOL 8. Develop an action plan

Based on each goal, identify tasks, who is responsible for each task, materials needed, and timeline for completing task.

TOOL 9. Develop a communication plan

What is the key information families need?
What feedback or input are we seeking from families?
Have we considered how diverse staff and families do or don't access district information?
Do we need to make our materials available in different languages?
Who will be responsible for communicating with parents?

TOOL 10. Evaluate family engagement annually

List family engagement activities developed in steps listed above. Collect evidence on effectiveness of family engagement, which can include surveys, interviews, focus groups, observations, student records, and records related to school leadership meetings.

District Focus on Family and Community Engagement

School districts throughout the state have established a variety of ways for parents, community members, community organizations, and businesses to become an integral part of the school and district functioning as well as to share in the educational opportunities with parents and communities. School districts have developed a variety of ways to share information for parents and community members. The district, in particular, is small enough to understand the needs of the community, while also large enough to be able to fund and provide parent and community engagement programs.

Local Control Accountability Plan (LCAP)

In response to two educational trends—accountability and local governance (*see Chapter Two for more discussion*)—California passed the Local Control Funding Formula (LCFF) (see Chapter Three), and with the LCFF came the requirement of a Local Control Accountability Plan (LCAP). School districts (Local Educational Agencies) must develop a plan that sets goals, lays out action plans to meet those goals, and utilize their resources to make sure that the goals are met for the purpose of improving student outcomes. As designated in Education Code 52060, all district-level LCAPs must include:

> (3) (A) Parental involvement and family engagement, including efforts the school district makes to seek parent input in making decisions for the school district and each individual schoolsite, and including how the school district will promote parental participation in programs for unduplicated pupils and individuals with exceptional needs.

> (B) Family engagement may include, but need not be limited to, efforts by the school district and each individual schoolsite to apply research-based practices, such as welcoming all families into the school community, engaging in effective two-way communication, supporting pupil success, and empowering families to advocate for equity and access. Family engagement may include, but need not be limited to, families as partners to inform, influence, and create practices and programs that support pupil success and collaboration with families and the broader community, expand pupil learning opportunities and community services, and promote civic participation.

As can be seen, LCAP requirements attempt to ensure that families are involved in all critical decisions about their children's schools.

District-Level Family and Community Engagement Strategies

In addition, school districts develop their own family and community engagement strategies to meet the particular needs and social climate of their communities. What follows here are several examples from across the state.

San Diego Unified School District. The San Diego Unified School District (https://www.sandiegounified.org/make-difference-get-involved-education) provides a welcoming message for families and communities on their district's webpage. Families and community members are welcomed with the message "Make a Difference—Get Involved w/Family And Community Engagement." Website viewers are introduced to the Office of Family and Community Engagement, with links to (a) Family Academic Learning Department, (b) Extended Learning Opportunities, (c) Youth and Family Advocacy Department, and (d) Partnerships and Community Engagement Department. Opportunities for families and community members to become involved are listed, including volunteering, serving on committees, and serving on the district's leadership team, among others. Visitors are further welcomed through the display of the district's Vision 2020:

> Vision 2020 highlights that involvement by parents, community members and the business community is essential to the success of San Diego Unified and its students. As we continue to create quality schools in every neighborhood and establish them as neighborhood learning centers, participation from our families, community members and business partners is more important and necessary than ever.

Finally, the San Diego Unified School District has also established the Harold J. Ballard Parent Center, which provides additional resources and services to parents including parent education, educational programs, and even provides childcare so that parents can participate in the events.

Bakersfield City School District. Bakersfield City School District (https://www.bcsd.com/apps/pages/index.jsp?uREC_ID=1066023&type=d&pREC_ID=1359627) welcomes families through its Family and Community Engagement website. Through this site, families can find a wide array of programs offered to help engage the schools with the families, including Parent University; Parent Groups; District Advisory Committee: District African American Parent Advisory Council; PALs (Parents As Leaders); a nutritional program titled "Now We're Cooking;" Father Engagement; and a Summer Parent Academy.

School-Level Focus on Family and Community Engagement

It is at the individual school level where families and communities are able to be most directly involved with the educational system, and it is where teachers can most directly become engaged and work with families and within the school's surrounding community.

Family Engagement

Commonly known types of family engagement include parent volunteers and parent-teacher organizations like PTA or PTO. In California, school-level committees provide the opportunity for parents to become involved in leadership and planning activities at their children's schools.

School Site Council. California law (Education Code 52852) requires that each school receiving supplemental funding based on a high percentage of socioeconomically disadvantaged students operate a School Site Council (SSC). Membership of an SSC must include the principal, teachers, parents, and in high schools, at least one student. SSC's take a strong leadership role in the operation of their schools, including developing and reviewing bylaws, making recommendations for the school's plans for increasing student achievement, and reviewing the school's budgets.

English Learner Advisory Committee. An English Learner Advisory Committee, popularly known as ELAC, is required by California law (Education Code 62002.5) in schools that have more than 20 English Learner students. ELAC has the same categories of membership as the SSC but exists for the main purpose of providing parents with the opportunity to have greater input into how the school addresses English Learner students, curriculum, and courses.

Community Engagement

There are many opportunities for schools to engage with community, for the purposes of drawing on community strengths to support K-12 education. A few examples include YMCA and Boys and Girls Clubs, community health clinics, places of worship, teen centers, and immigration assistance centers, among many others. Schools can also receive both financial and material support from businesses and groups within the community. Examples include donations by local businesses, support of programs such as sponsoring athletic teams or academic clubs, or donations of computers.

Issues of Equity and Social Justice

A look at two elementary schools in Sacramento, 1.2 miles away from each other, will show the impact of social and economic inequities on the level of community involvement with the schools (see Table 7.1). Leataata Floyd Elementary School serves almost entirely students from public housing ("the projects"), which means that nearly all families fall far below the poverty line, with 95.8% of students falling into the category of socioeconomically disadvantaged. Unique to this school is that it is named after long-time community member and matriarch of the public housing complex, Leataata Floyd. Located within walking distance is Crocker Riverside Elementary School, of which only 20.5% of students are socio-economically disadvantaged. Corresponding with this higher level of wealth, test scores are nearly 70% higher than test scores at Leataata Floyd. Indicative of the role of community wealth in providing opportunities for students, Crocker Riverside offers 11 programs for which parents must pay for their children to attend.

The community involvement with Leataata Floyd School is a common model in schools serving underprivileged children: community organizations provide free support services, and large corporations provide one-time donations, usually with no follow-up. Meanwhile, community involvement at Crocker Riverside is illustrative of the model at schools with community wealth: "enrichment" courses, paid for by parents, set students on a path to college, and these opportunities do not exist at schools serving a high percentage of underprivileged children such as Leataata Floyd School (*see Table 7.1 on page 109*).

Reflective and Action-Based Questions

1. *Examine one school's engagement with the community and list the activities. Describe whether the school has the support of community organizations providing free supportive services, corporations providing one time donations, parents paying for programs, or a combination of these. Discuss whether these activities are based on the models described above for either underprivileged schools or schools with community wealth.*
2. *Following the steps in the Family Engagement Toolkit previously laid out, work with a team to develop a draft of a family engagement plan for your school.*
3. *Locate the Local Control Accountability Plan for your district. Summarize three parent engagement activities described in the plan.*
4. *Despite a variety of support programs and policies that intend to involve all families, many are still left out of the decision-making process. Discuss two possible reasons why this may be the case.*

Table 7.1 - Impact of Socioeconomic Status on a School's Community Engagement

	Leataata Floyd	Crocker Riverside
% Socio-economically disadvantaged	95.8%	20.5%
Students of Color	98.9%	44.9%
Meeting Math State Standards	5%	73%
Community Engagement—offered free of charge by school	□ Before-and-after school program—Leataata Floyd Polynesian Dance	□ Art docent—parent volunteers □ Garden docent—parent volunteers □ Science docent—parent volunteers □ Running Club—parent volunteers
Community Engagement—offered free of charge by community organization	□ Before-and-after school program – Roberts Family Development Center □ City Year—outside volunteers from an AmeriCorps program (similar to Peace Corps, but in the U.S.)	□ n/a
Community Engagement—offered free due to sponsorship by corporation	□ Family computer center—sponsored by the NBA team Sacramento Kings □ Community garden—funding donated by Target stores	□ n/a
Community Engagement—parents pay for students to participate in program	□ n/a	□ Before-and-after school program—4th R, a Sacramento city program □ School Choir—parents pay for this program, offered by the school □ Orchestra—parents pay for this program, offered by the school □ Backyard Art Academy—parents pay for this program, offered by a community member □ Chess Club—parents pay for this program, offered by a community member □ Early Engineers—offered by a community organization □ Firefly Art—parents pay for this program, offered by an outside organization □ Honey Code (beginning coding)—parents pay for this program, offered by an outside organization □ Mad Science—parents pay for this program, offered by an outside organization □ Ninja Pandas—parents pay for this program, offered by an outside organization □ Young Actors Stage—parents pay for this program, offered by an outside organization

CHAPTER EIGHT

The Teaching Profession, California Style

Guiding Questions

1. *What are the steps required to earn a preliminary teaching credential in California?*
2. *How long does it take to earn a "clear credential?"*
3. *How do candidates find and apply for teaching positions?*

Introduction

Teaching children and adolescents is not for the faint of heart! Teachers are special people who have a combination of intelligence, thoughtfulness, perseverance, respect for others, energy, creativity, and a desire to help children, families, and society. The state of California, in its "Education Code," describes what it believes should make up a teacher (*see Figure 8.1*).

Figure 8.1 - How California Describes a Teacher

Teachers

- are academically talented.
- are knowledgeable of the subjects to be taught in the classroom.
- are creative and energetic.
- have the human skills to motivate and inspire pupils to achieve their goals.
- have the sensitivity to foster self-esteem in pupils through recognition that each pupil has his or her own goals, talents, and levels of development.
- are willing to relate the educational process and their instructional strategies to meet pupils' needs.
- are able to work effectively with and motivate pupils from a variety of ethnic, socioeconomic, cultural, academic, and linguistic backgrounds.
- have an understanding of principles and laws related to educational equity, and the equitable practice of the profession of education among all pupils regardless of their ethnicity, race, gender, age, religious background, primary language, or handicapping condition.

(*California Education Code*, section 44225)

It is likely that as you read this book you are either currently in a teacher credentialing program or are teaching or working in an educational setting. This chapter will take you through the process of getting a teaching credential, becoming a teacher, and continuing your learning as a teacher.

The Beginnings of Teacher Preparation in California

If there weren't free, public schools statewide until 1866, how did teachers become educated? Many of the state's first teachers either came from other states, where they had attended either universities or teacher training schools, or they were from Mexican or other Spanish-speaking traditions. In order to be able to educate California's teachers within California, the first school for teacher preparation called the State Normal School was opened in San Francisco in 1862, with 34 students training to become teachers.

California was involved early in the tradition of requiring teachers to pass an examination in order to receive their teaching certificate. School districts and Boards of Education were given the power to grant certificates "of good moral character and fitness to teach a common school *one year*" (Swett, 1876, p. 171). In the early days of this testing, the examiners could come from any profession, and often included people such as lawyers and barbers. After a battle with the legislators in charge of the teacher testing, Swett, in his Second Biennial Report of 1866–1867, described how this practice of examination was changed to better represent the nature of teaching:

> California is the only State in the Union in which teachers have gained the legal right to be examined exclusively by the members of their own profession, and we have just cause to be proud of the fact. It has already done much to make the occupation of teaching respectable. It has relieved good teachers from useless annoyance and humiliation; it has increased their self-respect, stimulated their ambition, and guarded the schools against quacks and pretenders.

The state teachers' examination of 1876 included subject matter questions in the following areas: Orthography, Grammar, Written Arithmetic, Geography, Reading, Defining, Mental Arithmetic, Oral Grammar, History of the United States, Composition, Penmanship, Algebra, Natural Philosophy, Physiology,

Natural History, Constitution of United States and California, School Laws of California, Industrial Drawing, and Vocal Music. There was a section on "Methods of Teaching" addressing pedagogical issues, as well as questions that asked teachers to critically reflect on the curriculum and pedagogy currently being practiced in the state.

Teachers in California in the 1860s were able to become part of the community of teachers throughout the state by receiving a state-wide teachers' journal—*California Teacher*—and annual State Institutes, which would currently be called either a convention or a conference in which educational issues are addressed. Topics addressed at these yearly institutes included adoption of a state set of textbooks, discussion of pedagogical strategies, school discipline, state taxes to support public education, school law, comparing education in Europe and America, moral training, and various other subject matter sessions.

The Teaching Credential

The path to becoming a teacher in California is not always a straight line. Beginning with a bachelor's degree, through to the gaining of the teaching credential, there is a mix of college or university courses, degrees, experiences in K-12 schools, and examinations. The path is not so much a sequential flowchart of steps to take, but rather a set of experiences through which a future teacher must pass. Over 75 colleges and universities throughout the state of California are authorized by the state to provide teacher credential programs, and these programs are designed to assist the candidate in successfully navigating through this series of requirements. Several additional pathways to the teaching credential include national models such as Teach for America and local models of partnership between districts and universities.

Credentials, Licenses, and Authorizations

The California Commission on Teacher Credentialing (CCTC) was established to serve as the umbrella organization for all matters and programs related to teacher credentialing within the state. Although each college or university that operates a teacher preparation program has its own unique character, each one also must fulfill the requirements set out by the CCTC (*see Figure 8.2 on page 114*).

FIGURE 8.2 - CALIFORNIA COUNCIL ON TEACHING CREDENTIALING

California Commission on Teacher Credentialing
www.ctc.ca.gov

Vision: To ensure that those who educate the children of this state are academically and professionally prepared.

Mission: To promote educational excellence and assure that the children of the State of California have fully qualified individuals to provide them with instruction and guidance.

The basic credential that is the first to be received is called the "Preliminary Credential," and can either be a Multiple Subject Teaching Credential or a Single Subject Teaching Credential. The Preliminary Credential is valid for five years, during which time a teacher must prepare for receiving the "Clear Credential. " The path to either the single subject or multiple subject preliminary credential includes the following components.

Preliminary Credential

The basic credential that is the first to be received is called the "Preliminary Credential," and can either be a Multiple Subject Teaching Credential or a Single Subject Teaching Credential. See *Figure 8.3* for a list of the subjects in which teachers can earn their Single Subject Teaching Credential.

FIGURE 8.3 - SINGLE SUBJECT CREDENTIAL AREAS

Agriculture	Mathematics
Art	Music
Business	Physical Education
English	Science: Biological Sciences
Foundational-Level General Science*	Science: Chemistry
Foundational-Level Mathematics	Science: Geosciences
Health Sciences	Science: Physics
Home Economics	Social Science
Industrial and Technology Education	World Language: English Language Development
	World Language: Languages other than English

*Foundational-level refers to a credential that would allow teachers to teach either General Science or Mathematics at an early level, such as in middle school or early high school. In Mathematics, this would allow a teacher to teach up through Advanced Algebra, for instance. For those wanting to teach the full range of Mathematics, the Mathematics credential is the correct option. In Sciences, the Foundational-Level General Science credential allows the teaching of general science through 12th grade. For the specialized sciences, teachers need one of the four Science credentials in the areas listed above.

The Preliminary Credential is valid for five years, during which time a teacher must prepare for receiving the "Clear Credential." The path to either the single subject or multiple subject preliminary credential includes the following components.

FIGURE 8.4 - REQUIREMENTS FOR PRELIMINARY TEACHING CREDENTIAL

Coursework	Examinations
Bachelor's Degree	California Basic Education Skills Test (CBEST)
Teacher Preparation Program	Reading Instruction Competence Assessment (RICA)
Course on Developing English Skills	California Subject Examinations for Teachers (CSET)
Course including the U.S. Constitution (or exam)	
Foundational Computer Technology Course	

**Note that this is not a complete list, but rather the main categories of requirements. See your own teacher credential program to discuss the full set of requirements further.*

Authorizations

Authorizations are available in most subject areas, Bilingual Education, and Special Education. Because authorizations are over and above the basic credential, they require additional coursework and examinations. Therefore, it is recommended, but not required, that students in a teaching credential program identify to their college or university their interest in earning an authorization either upon application or early in the teaching credential program. However, practicing teachers may also earn authorizations through additional courses and examinations, even while they are teaching. See the CCTC website for further information about available authorizations.

The Teaching Position

When entering the teaching profession for the first time, there is a flurry of paperwork that must be approved from the CCTC. However, most universities and colleges have offices that assist in the CCTC credentialing paperwork process.

Applying

Once prospective teachers have received their credential and any authorizations, there are many choices in location and type of school where they may choose to teach.

- **Public K-12**— apply through the school district.
- **Charter**—check the website of the individual charter school where you may want to apply. Some charters are independently operated, not part of the school district, and therefore will have their own application process. Some charter schools are included in a school district, and then you will find their openings on that district's site.
- **Private**— each school will have its own application process.

The California County Superintendents Educational Services Association provides assistance for new or veteran teachers looking for teaching positions. Through their "EdJoin" website (https://www.edjoin.org/), they provide information about open positions and teacher recruiting events. While some of the larger school districts throughout the state have their own online job application portal, some of the smaller districts utilize EdJoin as their online application service.

Professional Development

Teachers are strongly encouraged to participate in professional development, alternately called professional learning, in order to keep up with the most current theory and practice within the field. In fact, within the first years of holding the Preliminary Credential, teachers are provided with an "induction" process, where they are mentored by a veteran teacher who can help them in their new job.

The CDE hosts many professional development training sessions in specific areas where a need has been identified. For instance, there are a series of workshops on understanding and utilizing assessment, as well as professional development support for educators to provide equitable instruction to meet the needs of all learners. Many California school districts have an approved list of workshops that will fulfill any professional development requirement.

Collective Bargaining

Teachers in California are represented by very strong collective bargaining units, otherwise known as unions. There are two national teachers' unions that have California branches, as well as local school district unions. Teachers are not required to join a union, but the following describes the actions the unions take on behalf of all teachers and their students.

Now 150 years old, the California Teachers Association (CTA) was founded in 1863 to serve the professional needs of teachers. It is linked to the National Education Association. In addition to bargaining for teacher salaries, retirement, and health and other benefits, CTA develops policy briefs and organizes events to highlight the importance of K-12 education. CTA also argues at the State Capitol in favor of or against laws that will either strengthen or diminish the importance of K-12 schools and teachers.

The American Federation of Teachers (AFT) has been in existence since 1916, with more than 3,000 local affiliates from around the country. There are 65 local affiliates throughout California, including representing K-12, community colleges, and universities and colleges. AFT does similar work to that of the CTA, advocating for teachers, students, and the educational system in general.

Issues of Equity and Social Justice

The Introduction to this book presented the data on the number and percentage of students of color compared to teachers of color. There is certainly a mismatch. A strong case can be made for increasing the number of well-prepared K-12 teachers, in general, but especially new teachers of color. Numerous studies point to how students have a more positive experience in school when their teachers share their race and ethnicity. This includes greater academic, personal, and social success (Villegas & Irvine, 2010) and a positive experience that affirms students' ethnic identity, rather than stripping away their culture, language, or history. In this way, their ethnicity "becomes a source of strength" (Mercado, 2016, p. 30). At the same time, this does not discount the valuable role of White teachers. The key is to prepare culturally competent teachers who will respect and value all students' identities, languages, cultures, and histories.

One example of such a program is NLERAP (National Latino Education Research Agenda Project), which is based on research and best practices for preparing culturally and linguistically competent teachers (Nieto et al., 2012; Valenzuela, 2016). NLERAP principles aim to (a) affirm and build upon the linguistic and cultural heritage of Latinx and bilingual students, and (b) nurture Latinx students through high school and into a teacher preparation pathway that ultimately returns them back to their communities as teachers to empower the next generation. NLERAP also encourages a "grow your own" approach to preparing teachers for the diversity of today's California schools. If someone wants to be a teacher to serve their own community, then we are "growing" teachers from their own communities, who will go back to inspire and empower their own community members through education.

Reflective and Action-Based Questions

1. *Reflect on and write about why you want to be a teacher.*
2. *Develop two or three ideas for how you can go into a community, as a teacher, to mentor and empower K-12 students.*
3. *If you could suggest topics for ongoing professional development, what would be your top three, and why?*

References

Mercado, C. I. (2016). Teacher capacities for Latino and Latina youth. In A. Valenzuela (Ed.), *Growing critically conscious teachers: A social justice curriculum for educators of Latino/a youth*. New York: Teachers College Press.

Nieto, S., Rivera, M., & Irizarry, J. (2012). The NLERAP approach. *Association of Mexican-American Educators Journal, 6*(3), 7–9.

Swett, J. (1876). *History of the public school system in California*. San Francisco: A. L. Bancroft.

Valenzuela, A. (Ed.). (2016). *Growing critically conscious teachers: A social justice curriculum for educators of Latino/a youth*. New York: Teachers College Press.

Villegas, A. M., & Irvine, J. J. (2010). Diversifying the teaching force: An examination of major arguments. *The Urban Review, 42*, 175–192.

Appendix A

Education Code

http://leginfo.legislature.ca.gov/faces/codesTOCSelected.xhtml?tocCode=EDC

Education Code

California's education system (including K-12, community colleges, and higher education) is regulated by the "Education Code" (Ed Code), a very large and ever-evolving set of over 100,000 policies regulating schools. The website http://leginfo.legislature.ca.gov/faces/codesTOCSelected.xhtml?tocCode=EDC allows for a search of the Ed Code for any laws of particular interest. Reviewing the Ed Code is a very good way to learn about the thousands of laws that govern education in California.

The Ed Code is presented in three sections, with the numbers corresponding to the numbers of provisions in each section.

1. General Education Code Provisions [1–32500]
2. Elementary and Secondary Education [33000–64100]
3. Postsecondary Education [66000–101060]

Ed Code is organized by Title, Part, Chapter, Article, and then Provision number. The following is a sample of the outline of provisions, from the General Education section, with a special focus on Educational Equity and the Safe Place to Learn Act.

PART 1. GENERAL PROVISIONS 1-446

CHAPTER 1. General Provisions 1-95

CHAPTER 2. Educational Equity 200-262.4

ARTICLE 1. Declaration of Purpose 200-201

ARTICLE 2. Definitions 200-214

ARTICLE 2.5. Pupil and Student Suicide Prevention Policies 215-216

ARTICLE 3. Prohibition of Discrimination 220-221.1

ARTICLE 3.5. The California Racial Mascots Act 221.2-221.3

ARTICLE 4. Sex Equity in Education Act 221.5-231.5

ARTICLE 4.5. Single Gender Schools and Classes 232-232.6

ARTICLE 5. Hate Violence Prevention Act 233-233.8

ARTICLE 5.5. Safe Place to Learn Act 234-234.5
(Article 5.5 added by Stats. 2007, Ch. 566, Sec. 2.)

234.
(a) This article shall be known, and may be cited, as the Safe Place to Learn Act.
(b) It is the policy of the State of California to ensure that all local educational agencies continue to work to reduce discrimination, harassment, violence, intimidation, and bullying. It is further the policy of the state to improve pupil safety at schools and the connections between pupils and supportive adults, schools, and communities.
(Amended by Stats. 2011, Ch. 723, Sec. 1. (AB 9) Effective January 1, 2012. Operative July 1, 2012, by Sec. 8 of Ch. 723.)

234.1.
The department, pursuant to subdivision (b) of Section 64001, shall monitor adherence to the requirements of Chapter 5.3 (commencing with Section 4900) of Division 1 of Title 5 of the California Code of Regulations and this chapter as part of its regular monitoring and review of local educational agencies, commonly known as the Categorical Program Monitoring process. The department shall assess whether local educational agencies have done all of the following:
(a) Adopted a policy that prohibits discrimination, harassment, intimidation, and bullying based on the actual or perceived characteristics set forth in Section 422.55 of the Penal Code, including immigration status, and Section 220 of this code, and disability, gender, gender

identity, gender expression, nationality, race or ethnicity, religion, sexual orientation, or association with a person or group with one or more of these actual or perceived characteristics. The policy shall include a statement that the policy applies to all acts related to school activity or school attendance occurring within a school under the jurisdiction of the superintendent of the school district.
(b) Adopted a process for receiving and investigating complaints of discrimination, harassment, intimidation, and bullying based on any of the actual or perceived characteristics set forth in Section 422.55 of the Penal Code, including immigration status, and Section 220 of this code, and disability, gender, gender identity, gender expression, nationality, race or ethnicity, religion, sexual orientation, or association with a person or group with one or more of these actual or perceived characteristics. The complaint process shall include, but not be limited to, all of the following:
(1) A requirement that, if school personnel witness an act of discrimination, harassment, intimidation, or bullying, they shall take immediate steps to intervene when safe to do so.
(2) A timeline to investigate and resolve complaints of discrimination, harassment, intimidation, or bullying that shall be followed by all schools under the jurisdiction of the school district.
(3) An appeal process afforded to the complainant should he or she disagree with the resolution of a complaint filed pursuant to this section.
(4) All forms developed pursuant to this process shall be translated pursuant to Section 48985.
(c) Publicized antidiscrimination, anti-harassment, anti-intimidation, and antibullying policies adopted pursuant to subdivision (a), including information about the manner in which to file a complaint, to pupils, parents, employees, agents of the governing board, and the general public. The information shall be translated pursuant to Section 48985.
(d) (1) Provided, incident to the publicizing described in subdivision (c), to certificated schoolsite employees who serve pupils in any of grades 7 to 12, inclusive, who are employed by the local educational agency, information on existing schoolsite and community resources related to the support of lesbian, gay, bisexual, transgender, and questioning (LGBTQ) pupils, or related to the support of pupils who may

face bias or bullying on the basis of religious affiliation, or perceived religious affiliation.
(2) As used in this subdivision, both of the following apply:
(A) Schoolsite resources may include, but are not limited to, peer support or affinity clubs and organizations, safe spaces for LGBTQ or other at-risk pupils, counseling services, staff who have received antibias or other training aimed at supporting these pupils or who serve as designated support to these pupils, health and other curriculum materials that are inclusive of, and relevant to, these pupils, online training developed pursuant to Section 32283.5, and other policies adopted pursuant to this article, including related complaint procedures.
(B) Community resources may include, but are not limited to, community-based organizations that provide support to LGBTQ or other at-risk pupils and their families, and physical and mental health providers with experience or training in treating or supporting these pupils.
(e) Posted the policy established pursuant to subdivision (a) in all schools and offices, including staff lounges and pupil government meeting rooms.
(f) Maintained documentation of complaints and their resolution for a minimum of one review cycle.
(g) Ensured that complainants are protected from retaliation and that the identity of a complainant alleging discrimination, harassment, intimidation, or bullying remains confidential, as appropriate.
(h) Identified a responsible local educational agency officer for ensuring school district or county office of education compliance with the requirements of Chapter 5.3 (commencing with Section 4900) of Division 1 of Title 5 of the California Code of Regulations and this chapter.
(i) Nothing in this section shall be construed to require school employees to engage with religious institutions in the course of identifying community support resources pursuant to this section.
(Amended by Stats. 2017, Ch. 493, Sec. 4. (AB 699) Effective January 1, 2018.)

234.2.
(a) The department shall display current information, and periodically update information, on curricula and other resources that specifically address bias-related discrimination, harassment,

intimidation, cyber sexual bullying, as defined in Section 48900, and bullying based on any of the actual or perceived characteristics set forth in Section 422.55 of the Penal Code and Section 220 on the California Healthy Kids Resource Center Internet Web site and other appropriate department Internet Web sites where information about discrimination, harassment, intimidation, cyber sexual bullying, and bullying is posted.

(b) The department shall annually inform school districts of the information on the California Healthy Kids Resource Center Internet Web site and other appropriate department Internet Web sites where information about cyber sexual bullying is posted pursuant to subdivision (a). The department may use electronic mail to inform school districts of this information.

(c) School districts are encouraged to inform pupils regarding the available information and resources on the department's Internet Web sites regarding the dangers and consequences of cyber sexual bullying to help reduce the instances of cyber sexual bullying.

(Amended by Stats. 2016, Ch. 419, Sec. 1. (AB 2536) Effective January 1, 2017.)

234.3.

The department shall develop a model handout describing the rights and obligations set forth in Sections 200, 201, and 220 and the policies addressing bias-related discrimination, harassment, intimidation, and bullying in schools. This model handout shall be posted on appropriate department Internet Web sites.

(Amended by Stats. 2011, Ch. 723, Sec. 4. (AB 9) Effective January 1, 2012. Operative July 1, 2012, by Sec. 8 of Ch. 723.)

234.4.

(a) A local educational agency shall adopt, on or before December 31, 2019, procedures for preventing acts of bullying, including cyberbullying.

(b) For purposes of this section, a "local educational agency" means a school district, a county office of education, or a charter school.

(Added by Stats. 2018, Ch. 491, Sec. 1. (AB 2291) Effective January 1, 2019.)

234.5.

(a) The Superintendent shall post, and annually update, on the department's Internet Web site and provide to each school district a list of statewide resources, including community-based organizations, that provide support to youth, and their families, who have been subjected to school-based discrimination, harassment, intimidation, or bullying, including school-based discrimination, harassment, intimidation, or bullying on the basis of religious affiliation, nationality, race, or ethnicity, or perceived religious affiliation, nationality, race, or ethnicity.
(b) The department's Internet Web site shall also include a list of statewide resources for youth who have been affected by gangs, gun violence, and psychological trauma caused by violence at home, at school, and in the community.
(Amended by Stats. 2016, Ch. 621, Sec. 3. (AB 2845) Effective January 1, 2017.)

ARTICLE 5.7. Pupil Protections Relating to Immigration and Citizenship Status 234.7

ARTICLE 6. Alternative Schools, Charter Schools, and School Choice 235

ARTICLE 7. Instructional Materials 240-241

ARTICLE 8. Compliance 250-253

ARTICLE 9. Enforcement 260-262.4

CHAPTER 3. English Language Education for Immigrant Children 300-340

CHAPTER 5. English Language Learner Acquisition and Development Pilot Program 420-421

CHAPTER 6. English Learner and Immigrant Pupil Federal Conformity Act 430-446

[The Ed Code continues this way through number 101060.]

Appendix B

California Department of Education

https://www.cde.ca.gov/

California Department of Education

The CDE website provides comprehensive information on how California addresses many of the topics covered within this book: https://www.cde.ca.gov/. The website provides details on many topics, along with updated lists of events, news releases about California's schools, and highlighted stories. The site presents written materials as well as videos, and provides social media outlets for those interested in California education. The following is a listing of the key topics addressed, with a focus on Learning Support.

Curriculum & Instruction

- Career Technical Education
- Curriculum Resources
- Grade Spans
- Professional Learning
- Subject Areas

Testing & Accountability

- Accountability
- Compliance Monitoring
- District & School Interventions
- Awards and Recognition
- Testing

Finance & Grants

- Accounting
- Allocations & Apportionments
- Funding
- Finance & Grants Other Topics

Data & Statistics

- Data Collections
- Financial
- Demographics

Student Health & Support

- Downloadable Data Files
- Data Requests
- School Identification
- School Performance

Specialized Programs

- Adult Education
- Charter Schools
- Child Development
- Educational Options
- English Learners
- Special Education
- Title I
- Specialized Programs Other Topics

Learning Support—"Provides resources and instructional strategies that give students the physical, social, emotional, and intellectual support needed to learn."

- Highlighted resources and guidelines provided
    - Bullying and Hate Motivated Behavior Prevention
    - Child Abuse Identification & Reporting Guidelines
    - Mental Health
    - Truancy
    - Homeless Education
    - Foster Youth Services

- Further learning support pages
    - Attendance Improvement
    - Before & After School
    - Counseling/Student Support
    - Education Technology
    - Facilities
    - Health
    - Nutrition

    - Parents/Family & Community
    - Safe Schools
    - Transportation
    - Youth Development

- What's New and What's Trending in Learning Support

The CDE website also provides links to critical topics for current and future educators as well as parents and communities, include State Board of Education meeting agendas and minutes, CDE job openings, Superintendent Initiatives, and multilingual documents covering a wide variety of California's education topics.

Appendix C

California Commission on Teacher Credentialing

https://www.ctc.ca.gov/

California Commission on Teacher Credentialing

The California Commission on Teaching Credentialing (CTC) provides information for (a) current and future teachers earning credentials and authorizations, (b) teacher preparation programs within the state, and (c) employers. It also allows for reporting of educator misconduct, and it provides reports and data on the current state of teaching within California. For current and future educators, a series of steps allows potential recipients to learn about accreditation, apply for, and check on the status of their application for a credential or authorization. For those educated within an accredited California teacher preparation program, their programs take the responsibility for ensuring that applicants understand the process of receiving a credential or authorization. The CTC website lays out the path to credentials.

1. Educator: Complete Approved Program
2. Program Sponsor (college or university providing the teacher preparation program): Submit formal online recommendation to the CTC on behalf of their program completers
3. Educator: Complete Online Recommendation (within 90 days of completing teacher preparation program)
4. CTC: Process Credential Recommendation

Applicants can check the status of their credential or authorization application at any time with the online system provided by the CTC.

Finally, the CTC website provides an avenue for the public to "Search for an Educator." By simply typing in a potential educator's name, information is visible such as credentials or authorizations earned by the educator. Thus the CTC is the location for all official documents related to each educator's credential or authorization.

Author Bio

Jana Noel is Professor of Education at California State University, Sacramento (Sacramento State) and former (2012–2013) American Council on Education Fellow. She received her Ph.D. from UCLA in 1991, and her expertise is in urban teacher education, multicultural education, university-school-community partnerships, and foundations of education. She has published numerous articles and several books, has received both research and service awards, and serves as Associate Editor of the journal *Issues in Teacher Education*. Dr. Noel's 2013 book, *Moving Teacher Education into Urban Schools and Communities: Prioritizing Community Strengths* (Routledge), received a national Critics Choice award from the American Educational Studies Association, and her Urban Teacher Education Center (which moved a teacher education program into a school serving public housing), was honored with a 2008 Quality Education Partnership Award for Distinguished Service to Children and the Preparation of Teachers, given by the California Council on Teacher Education. While serving as the Sacramento State Director of Educational and Community Research Partnerships (2015–2018), Dr. Noel assisted in generating over $13 million in grant funding for university students, faculty, staff, and K-12 and community partners.

Index